Empty Bed Blues

and

The Fox... and the Little Vixen

Stephen Lowe

with an Afterword by John Worthen

Critical, Cultural and Communications Press
in association with the D. H. Lawrence Research Centre,
University of Nottingham

Nottingham

2010

Nottingham Lawrence Studies
General editors: Sean Matthews and Macdonald Daly

Empty Bed Blues and *The Fox... and the Little Vixen*, by Stephen Lowe.

First published in Great Britain by Critical, Cultural and Communications Press in association with the D. H. Lawrence Research Centre, University of Nottingham, 2010.

Author's agent: **Howard Gooding, Judy Daish Associates, 2. St. Charles Place, London W10 6EG (tel. +44 (0)208 964 8811).**

Cover design by Andrew Dawson.

ISBN 9781905510283

Contents

About the author

Nottingham-born and Nottingham-based Stephen Lowe has written over fifty plays for the theatre including the award-winning *Touched* (directed by Richard Eyre); *Comic Pictures* (directed by Alan Ayckbourn); *The Ragged Trousered Philanthropists* (for Joint Stock directed by Bill Gaskill and then Stratford East directed by Stephen Daldry); *Glasshouses, Tibetan Inroads* (Royal Court); and *Divine Gossip* (RSC). His TV/Film work includes the BBC Classic Serial, *Scarlet and Black*, starring Ewan McGregor; BAFTA-nominated thriller *Tell-Tale Hearts* and two BBC films set in Nottingham, directed by Alan Dossor: *Ice Dance* and *Flea Bites* (starring Nigel Hawthorne). Stephen has also written over a hundred episodes of *Coronation Street*. His 2006 play *Old Big 'Ead in the Spirit of the Man* (also directed by Alan Dossor) played to packed houses at the Nottingham Playhouse. He was a council member of Arts Council England and Chair of ACE-East Midlands. For more information, visit his website **www.stephenlowe.co.uk** and, for his theatre company, Meeting Ground, **www.meetingground.theatre.org.uk**.

About Nottingham Lawrence Studies

The D. H. Lawrence Research Centre at the University of Nottingham was founded in 1990 to provide a focus for research and teaching in Lawrence Studies, and to promote the Lawrence Collections. The Centre hosts conferences, symposia and lectures, as well as coordinating Lawrence-related classes and courses at undergraduate and postgraduate level. We also work closely with Lawrence Societies around the world, particularly the Eastwood D. H. Lawrence Society, and offer support for Visiting Scholars wishing to use the Lawrence Collections. Nottingham Lawrence Studies was established in 2008 to publish work in the field. We welcome submissions, and proposals, of work of interest to academics, students and general readers. These should be sent to:

The D. H. Lawrence Research Centre
School of English Studies
University of Nottingham
University Park
Nottingham
United Kingdom
NG7 2RD

Empty Bed Blues

In 1929, D. H. Lawrence and his wife visited two wealthy young Americans, hoping they might finance an edition of *Lady Chatterley's Lover*. The events of this weekend are drawn directly from the personal diaries, letters and writings of all four of the participants.

A rehearsed reading of *Empty Bed Blues* took place at the 2007 International D. H. Lawrence Conference in Eastwood.

The first performance of *Empty Bed Blues* was given at the Djanogly Theatre, Lakeside Arts Centre, Nottingham, on 6 March 2009 by Lakeside Arts in partnership with Lincoln Performing Arts Centre.

The cast was as follows:

D. H. Lawrence – Tim Dantay
Frieda Lawrence – Marion Bailey
Harry Crosby – Tristan Tait
Caresse Crosby – Claire Calbraith

Director – Matt Aston
Designer – Mark Walters
Digital Media Designer – Barret Hodgson
Lighting Design – Ciaran Bagnall
Sound Design – Drew Baumohl

Characters

D. H. Lawrence, 43, English
Frieda Lawrence, 49, German
Harry Crosby, 30, Boston American
Caresse Crosby, 36, New York American
A parrot

The time – Easter, 1929

The place – Moulin du Soleil, Northern France

Caresse Crosby

Harry Crosby

D. H. Lawrence

Frieda Lawrence

Act One

Scene One

The Magic Pool.

Darkness. Almost jungle sounds, parrots calling, dogs barking, strange cries. A shadowy pool on a cold, grey day. A mist hovers over it. A few benches that have almost been taken over by the undergrowth. LAWRENCE carefully weaves his way through the trees. Now a frail forty-three, in his traditional tight white jacket, hat and leather shoulder bag. He stops to listen to the sounds. He frowns, curious. He takes in the pool. He stares down at the scattered items of a man's evening wear. A "raccoon" coat lies splayed out like a sleeping bear. LAWRENCE gingerly toes it, half expecting it to pounce.

LAWRENCE: Dead. Praise the Lord.

A strange animal cry cuts the air. Then silence. He looks around, coughs politely by way of introducing himself, gains no response, frowns, smiles to himself, then this time coughs unwillingly for a moment. He recovers, wipes his mouth with a handkerchief, checks it, nods, and puts it away. He wipes his forehead with the back of his hand and studies that too. Then —

LAWRENCE: (*Overplaying his native accent*) What's th' doin' ere, Bertie old lad? (*Sits: sighs*) Daft bloody question. (*As normal*) What am I doing here? What do I ever do? (*Opens his satchel and takes out his notebook*) (*Reading and amending*) *The Escaped Cock* by D. H. Lawrence. Jesus, they'll ban it just for the title alone. And then they'll definitely crucify you after they've read it. Still…. Rather the point. Rather the point. Start with the crucifixion, and see how we go. (*Smiles*) Hm. "There was a peasant near Jerusalem who acquired a young gamecock which looked a shabby little thing, but which put on fine feathers" – no – "put on *brave* feathers as spring advanced, and was resplendent with arched and orange neck by the time the fig-trees were letting out leaves from their end-tips." Yes.

(*Coughs*) Hm. Yes. (*Mumbling on as he revises*) Certain beauty? "The cock grew to a certain beauty"… no, more than beauty… (*With relish*) splendour. Yes. Splendour. "He is a game game-cock. He is good for twenty hens, said the wife." (*Triumphant*) Yes. So, Bertie, we start, we have a tale here to tell. But can we make it to the end? (*Sighs*) Or will the mist — the sea mist — will the sea mist take us first?

LAWRENCE *quietly returns to his work. Suddenly a naked young man bursts up and out of the pond. HARRY CROSBY, with boyish good looks, and indeed great boyish charm. He punches the air in triumph.*

HARRY: Ra! Ra!

HARRY's *accent is light, crisp, that of the aristocratic Bostonian Yankee. He laughs, shivers and shakes himself like some golden Labrador. He realises someone is watching. He turns to* LAWRENCE.

HARRY: Oh. Jesus Christ!

LAWRENCE: Well, not according to the *Daily Telegraph*.

HARRY: Oh, Lawrence? Lawrence. Sir. I… oh, my… it went completely… I completely… how could I, what can I say, I mean I've dreamed of this day to finally meet you and…

LAWRENCE: (*Mildly*) Like so many dreams, forgotten in a moment.

HARRY: Not this one, no sir. Not this one. (*Grins at Lawrence*) Welcome, welcome. (*Offers his hand*)

LAWRENCE: Harry. You know, your wife has half of France out looking for you.

HARRY: Why does she do that? She knows, she understands, that some times, well, we all get lost don't we, that's part of the endless journey, it's into the unknown, of course you understand that better than anyone, it's in every word you write, that when night comes, there can be no denying the dark, no frail holding onto flickering candles, clinging to false shadows on the cave wall, when you and I, when we truly face the dark gods, what I call the Black Sun and you the Plumed Serpent, well then it's not just a matter of shaking hands, you just have to dive straight in.

LAWRENCE: (*Lightly*) Good idea to remember a towel though. Put this on, Harry, (*Offering up the coat*) before you catch your death.

HARRY: (*Quietly*) So you believe it too?

LAWRENCE: What?

HARRY: That one can catch death.

LAWRENCE: It's a figure of speech, Harry. The art is not to confuse poetry with life. They do not exactly twin.

HARRY: Unless one lives a life of poetry. Like you do. And perhaps…. I…

He shrugs, grins at LAWRENCE, *then takes the coat.* LAWRENCE *studies him as he slides into it.*

LAWRENCE: (*Gently*) And then what, Harry? When you have plunged into your particular black sun?

HARRY: You pray for startling resurrection. For the Sun to turn our baseness into gold again.

LAWRENCE: And how does this alchemy take place?

Act One

HARRY: Magic. (*Grins*) In this magic pool. It's why we bought the Moulin here. This is the sacred pool of the greatest magician the world has ever known, Count Cagliostro.

LAWRENCE: The man they say has never died?

HARRY: Oh, no, that's wrong, no, he dies all right, over and over again, but at each appointed time, and he knows the time, he returns to this black pool and surfaces again reborn. (*Smiling*) I keep champagne chilled in the lower depths ready for his next rebirth.

LAWRENCE: And will you recognise him when he arrives?

HARRY: (*Pause: Looking at* LAWRENCE) I think so. Yes.

Silence.

LAWRENCE: (*Lightly*) Some Easter tale, Harry.

HARRY: It's yours for free.

LAWRENCE: Thank you. But I am working on one of my own.

CARESSE CROSBY *and* FRIEDA *arrive.* CARESSE *is a beautiful, slight, 36 year-old with a soft, but distinct New York accent. She carries a wrapped "parasol/umbrella" as if in hope of sunny days.* FRIEDA *is 49, stout, carefree, and chain-smoking. Fluent, she still speaks with a deep and strong German accent. Brecht would have loved her as a singer.*

CARESSE: Harry! Where the hell have you been?

LAWRENCE: Just been having a little redemptive swim.

HARRY *kisses* CARESSE.

HARRY: Later, Caresse, sweet heart, right now… (*Turning to* FRIEDA) Mrs Lawrence, Frieda, may I call you that?… I must first sincerely apologise…. I fell amongst thieves you know and − (*As his coat is open*)

FRIEDA: (*Grinning*) Please. I don't see anything to apologise for.

CARESSE: Buttons, Harry.

HARRY: (*In no way embarrassed*) Oh, God, sorry.

LAWRENCE: Don't fret. Frieda has just returned from the black pools of Baden Baden. She's more than used to the sight of naked young men, aren't you, Frieda?

FRIEDA: But it is still a pleasure.

HARRY: I am so sorry, I had a whole speech of welcome prepared.

CARESSE: Just say hi, Harry.

HARRY: Oh, hell. Okay, hi.

FRIEDA: Come here, my beauty, now you are at least half decent. No man should ever be more than that.

She hugs him, and then stares into his face.

FRIEDA: You look like some ruby cheeked choir boy who sings psalms whilst his hand plays in his pocket.

HARRY: (*Laughing*) You got me in one. And you, are you one of those lost Catholic souls?

FRIEDA: No, no, I was good Prussian Protestant but my

parents sent me to a convent school. For better education. It was true. I learned all I know about sex from choirboys like you. And of course the occasional nun.

HARRY: Surely your husband has taught you a thing or two?

FRIEDA: Hm. (*Lightly*) Perhaps I taught him. And he simply wrote it down.

LAWRENCE: Beware your inspiration, Harry, for fear they bid for copyright.

FRIEDA: It is so beautiful here. What are we, an hour away from Paris, and yet we could be anywhere. In Italy. In a forest.

LAWRENCE: A jungle.

CARESSE: That's Harry. He's setting up a menagerie here.

FRIEDA: So many animals. And your dogs. Oh, I love that bitch of yours, Harry. (*Laughing*) I mean of course the dog.

CARESSE: Of course.

LAWRENCE: Strange name for a dog though. Clytoris.

CARESSE: I called her that because Harry can never find her at night.

A silence then Lawrence begins to laugh.

HARRY: (*Grinning*) Forgive my wife. Caresse is from Brooklyn. She doesn't know any better.

The laughing sets off a coughing bout.

CARESSE: You okay, Lawrence? Fetch you some water?

LAWRENCE: I'm perfectly... perfectly... it's partly the fresh air after Paris. Hits one as such a shock. But more than welcome.

CARESSE: You want we should go inside? Too chilly for you here.

LAWRENCE: No, no, actually I'm really quite, quite hot and besides I've been folded like a pen-knife over papers for days. I'm in need of a little stretching. And just a moment's rest.

He sits on the bench.

CARESSE: Perhaps when you are.... Maybe, Harry, later Lawrence might want to stroll down the stables with you?

HARRY: You interested in horses?

LAWRENCE: (*Carefully*) I once rode in a Derby. On a donkey at Skegness. I think I won. She was called Maud.

CARESSE: Harry has a beauty racing at Chantilly on Monday.

HARRY: My boy may not be up to Maud's level, but I have real hope.

FRIEDA: Come, Caresse, let us leave the men to talk of stallions. And leave us women to do the same.

There is a hesitance, a delicacy, between the two men. LAWRENCE *rises and begins to gather* HARRY's *clothes together. He hands the undergarments first to* HARRY. HARRY *nods.*

HARRY: Thank you.

HARRY *begins to dress properly, and* LAWRENCE *assists him like some well-trained butler brushing mud off his clothes.* LAWRENCE *is quietly enjoying it.*

LAWRENCE: This horse of yours, will it win?

HARRY: Oh, God, yes, no question he won't romp home. Sunstroke was born to pull the Sun God across the heavens. He's a top thorough-bred through and through.

LAWRENCE: (*Quietly*) How does one qualify as a thorough-bred, Harry?

HARRY: Simple question of breeding. All thorough-breds trace their ancestors from three Arabian stallions who in the seventeen century rogered the finest English mares. In 1730 the first thorough-bred stud called Bull Rock, or Rockballs as we call him, arrived on heat in America –

LAWRENCE: Almost with the Pilgrim Fathers.

HARRY: Not far behind. (*Smiling*) But with a somewhat different philosophy of sex.

LAWRENCE: And when did your ancestors arrive?

HARRY: Pretty much on the first boat.

LAWRENCE: So you're a kind of American thoroughbred, too, aren't you?

HARRY: (*Lightly*) 'Fraid so. The old Boston aristocracy.

LAWRENCE: It must be wonderful to be so confident that one is so thoroughly bred. (*Pause*) My father, who I loathed, would come home black and glittering with coal. My mother would wash him carbolic clean in a tin bath in front of the fire and she'd tremble and turn away as he rose pure white from the black pool as hunched all day underground he straightens now into his pride. And into his rage. His inarticulate rage against those who kept him tied, who forced his back to bend into submission. That spirit never buckled under him no matter how much he had to kneel. Was he, I wonder now, in his own way, a thorough-bred? She always doubted it. And I did too. (*Pause*) Perhaps I was wrong. Perhaps so are you − perhaps the true thorough-breds are chained, pit ponies driven under ground, spine compressed, but still capable in the light of day of straightening into pride, still resisting everything, resisting surrender, resisting death, still determined on "coming through!" Whilst the so-called thorough-bred stud is little more than a posh prick that comes erect at anyone's behest. Perhaps.

Silence. HARRY *is for once at a loss. Silence.* LAWRENCE *seems lost in thought.*

LAWRENCE: (*Mildly*) It's going to rain.

HARRY: Oh, no, no, that won't… I've personally done a deal with the sun-god Ra, especially for you. I *guarantee* the sun. I promise you, it's going to come bursting through.

LAWRENCE: (*Eventually*) Rain.

He strolls away. He leaves HARRY *half-dressed, the game now no longer of interest.*

HARRY: Come on, Ra. Sun. Sun. Don't you dare to betray me. Please.

He looks uncertain up into the sky. The first doubt of his faith. He turns, momentarily lost, then sets off in the direction of LAWRENCE.

Light change − "of the forest". As the women wander arm in arm −

CARESSE: You think those two will hit it off okay?

FRIEDA: It depends so much on the weather. Lorenzo is English remember. Pray it doesn't rain too hard. He goes wild then.

CARESSE: (*Carefully*) Is he a little difficult to live with?

FRIEDA: (*Simply*) He's my favourite child.

CARESSE: But you have other children?

FRIEDA: (*Pause*) They are grown up now of course. From my first marriage.

CARESSE: My daughter Polly she's sixteen now. My first marriage too.

FRIEDA: Does she visit?

CARESSE: (*Carefully*) Once in a blue moon. She and… well, she and Harry… he tries his best but… (*Pause*) I felt so guilty about deserting…

FRIEDA: Of course. It is not easy. How can it be? (*Pause*) But what can you do? We two have much in common. We choose to live by passion, and that comes with a price. My first husband, Professor Ernest Weekley, such a kind man, Lorenzo was his favourite student. Weekley was weakly, love was weakly and weekly love was not enough for me. Lorenzo made this play on words, it was cruel but it was true. I needed a younger man to ride me to the world and back again. It was the same for you?

CARESSE: (*Lightly*) You were right. We are talking of stallions.

FRIEDA *laughs. As* LAWRENCE *ambles towards them —*

CARESSE: Ah, there you are, Lawrence. Have you lost my husband?

LAWRENCE: He's fully capable of losing himself.

CARESSE: Don't I know?

FRIEDA: I was frightened for you with the woods here. Sometimes he comes over all pagan. You know, he strips and makes love to trees.

CARESSE: And how do they respond?

LAWRENCE: They're never complained.

FRIEDA: English trees are so polite, of course. But I once had to calm down a Canadian Pine from calling out the Mounties.

LAWRENCE: That was a slight misunderstanding. Could happen to anyone. (*Smiling*) It's splendid, really splendid out here, Caresse. I fully expect to see shimmering apples on the trees, and a snake to whisper temptation to me.

FRIEDA: We have snakes at home in Italy.

LAWRENCE: They tempt other people. But not me.

FRIEDA: (*Curious*) You still want to be tempted, Lorenzo?

LAWRENCE: I'd like a cup of tea.

FRIEDA: He likes it mashed.

CARESSE: Mashed?

FRIEDA: Boiled to death. Men must have it so thick you can stand a spoon erect in it.

Act One

HARRY appears, racoon coat over his shoulder but still keeping an eye out for the weather.

CARESSE: Harry? We're going in for tea. Before it rains.

HARRY: Who says it's going to rain?

FRIEDA: I want to see inside. To live in a moulin, a round house, to have no edges to cut yourself on. Like a fairy tale tower. (*Laughs*) Lorenzo has small tower like this where he writes in Italy. We have such a beautiful villa there.

LAWRENCE: Had.

FRIEDA: We must go back, my love. Everything we could need is there.

LAWRENCE: Everything you need… Besides, we can't run to it. The Italians put up the rent every time you step out the door. And right now, as you well know, we don't have two 'apennies to rub together.

CARESSE: You okay, Harry?

HARRY: Sure, why not?

FRIEDA: Just for one more year at least, Lorenzo. Please, for me. I want to be in the garden again. The hibiscus. The hibiscus calls to me.

A sudden sharp shriek, and a beating of wings

LAWRENCE: (*Startled*) What in −

FRIEDA: (*Pointing up*) Look, it's there, Lorenzo. In the tree.

LAWRENCE: You let your parrot fly free?

CARESSE: Tiresias would never leave.

LAWRENCE: Knows which side it's bread's buttered.

CARESSE: Sorry?

FRIEDA: A beauty.

LAWRENCE: It has a certain splendour.

HARRY: And talent, too. Come on, Tiresias, do your party piece, come on for daddy, eh?

PARROT: I cun't, ken you ninny? I cun't, ken you ninny?

LAWRENCE: What?

HARRY: Tiresias is the only parrot in the world who can quote James Joyce.

LAWRENCE: Well, that's a blessing.

CARESSE: He also lays eggs.

FRIEDA: He seems a trifle confused.

LAWRENCE: Wouldn't you be if you had to imitate a madman who imagines you become a revolutionary by simply inverting the Christian cross? God save us from such inanity.

HARRY: Well, that's a little extreme, Lawrence. I mean, whatever his faults and I admit they are legion, Joyce is undeniably a great writer. Everyone says that.

LAWRENCE: Everyone? How many parrots do you know?

HARRY: Well, if it bothers you so much I can easily get him to imitate you.

CARESSE: Harry!

HARRY: Oh, yes, no, I'm really sorry I didn't mean to be rude, I just –

LAWRENCE: (*Flaring into sudden fire*) I don't want imitations. Joyce may well do because in truth he doesn't have a real voice of his own, just some verbal tricks that even a parrot can mimic. A writer's voice is all he has. I am nothing but my voice. No one should possess my voice. All of you, find your own. Scrabble about in your own darkness, listen to the bitter whispers of your own soul, and spit them into the ear of the world. But be prepared to pay the cost, it's not bought with gold but blood, your very... (*Suddenly coughing, then slowly recovering but totally drained*)

HARRY: Can I get you –

FRIEDA: He should rest. It was a long drive.

LAWRENCE: I am not tired. I just need air. Need to walk. Walk. Walk.

FRIEDA: I'll come with you.

LAWRENCE: What for?

FRIEDA: Just in case –

LAWRENCE: (*As he goes: Still fighting for breath*) Don't pretend to be Florence fucking Nightingale. It ill becomes you.

LAWRENCE leaves. Silence.

HARRY: Did I say, or do...?

FRIEDA: You're sweet. No. I think I had best go after him.

CARESSE: Would you like an umbrella?

HARRY: It's not an umbrella. It's a parasol.

CARESSE: (*Carefully*) Whatever. It might do.

FRIEDA: Please.

HARRY: Should I not go?

FRIEDA: (*Gently*) Why? (*As she leaves*) Beautiful. Beautiful house. (*Pause*) Beautiful garden.

She goes. Silence.

CARESSE: What is it, Harry?

HARRY: (*Quietly*) I don't…. He's a great writer. Great. His words on a page, a man gets sunstroke reading them. I love… More than that. To me he's nothing less than a… But… (*Sighs*) This man, this great artist, this… he took it on himself to explain to me his host, his… he took it on himself to explain *to me* the true nature of a thorough-bred. This man who couldn't tell a Palomino from a pit-pony. This man who claims his ancestors, black shadows who constantly shunned the sun, he claims they are more thorough bred and true than….

Silence.

CARESSE: Does he disappoint you?

Silence.

HARRY: (*Pauses*) I just thought he would be taller.

He looks up at the sky. The first drops of rain.

CARESSE: Easter Sunday is tomorrow, Harry. Then there will be sun.

She gently takes his arm and leads him in. Darkness. The clouds suddenly burst. Heavy rain beating all around. It sends off a whole cacophony of howls and cries from a whole menagerie of animals. LAWRENCE soaking wet but apparently unconcerned stands listening – fascinated, fearful. FRIEDA seeks him.

FRIEDA: Lorenzo.

LAWRENCE: Listen. Listen. (*Pause*) What is this man running
   – a private jungle? Beware snakes. Lions. Tyger! Tyger!
   burning bright / in the forests of the night…

FRIEDA: Quoting other poets, not like you, Lorenzo.

LAWRENCE: Blake is dead.

FRIEDA: Oh, yes, of course. Come under the umbrella. You'll
   catch a fever.

LAWRENCE: I am a fever.

FRIEDA: What are you doing, my love?

LAWRENCE: I am being pissed on from a great height. That's
   fine. God, I prefer it to being pissed on by some self-
   appointed Pope of a playboy publisher.

FRIEDA: He's a fool, just a fool but he means no harm. The
   boy's nervous. Shy.

LAWRENCE: Shy? He practically waved his cock at you to say
   bonjour.

24 |

FRIEDA: Well, that's a little unusual, ja, I admit, but everyone tries to put their best foot forward?

LAWRENCE: Is that some kind of joke?

FRIEDA: Listen to me, my love, you said when you met me at the station that we are here for only one reason. Money. You reminded me these people once paid in gold coins to publish your beautiful tale called "Sun".

LAWRENCE: Only because its title was "Sun". The man is obsessed with his false God.

FRIEDA: So we re-name *Lady Chatterley's Lover* Lord Sun God Ra Ra Ra, what does it matter? We have no pennies, no mind the pounds. We must get your masterpiece published and God knows you have tried everywhere else. These are your last hope. Is that correct?

LAWRENCE: (*Reluctantly*) Yes.

FRIEDA: Then if that is so, perhaps this, the way you are, is not the best way to be.

LAWRENCE: How am I to be? Don't they know who I am ? God, the whole world knows. Or at least imagines it does.

FRIEDA: Come inside, Lorenzo. You're tired. Come rest. Sleep. Come with me, please. We have hardly spoke… I'm so worried for you. Please. Just come and lie down. Lie down with me, eh? It's been so long. (*Softly*) Lorenzo. Don't turn away. Please. Look at me. So. Now touch me. Love me. (*She moves to him*) Let me touch you.

LAWRENCE: Don't. Don't you dare touch me.

FRIEDA: Dare?

LAWRENCE: Stay away.

FRIEDA: (*Eventually*) (*Sighs*) It's all right, my love. I understand.

LAWRENCE: What do you understand?

FRIEDA: You are ill.

LAWRENCE: No.

FRIEDA: Yes, look at you now. More sweat than rain pouring down you. You shake like a leaf. You're having one of your… come, just come inside, rest lie down please. I'll look after you. I'll never leave you Lorenzo, no matter what, you know that.

LAWRENCE: (*Increasingly feverish*) There's nothing wrong with me. Nothing. How dare you offer me your… you have the nerve to pity me and play the loving angel. You who dream only of Baden Baden and being buoyed up in magic pools.

FRIEDA: What do you mean?

LAWRENCE: You think I don't know who that particular *boy* buoying you up is, or that when you drivel and dribble on and on about lying under hibiscus in your Tuscan paradise that I don't know *whose* that flesh-red hibiscus is, tumescent and ripe − that I can't see through your particular facile mask of poesy to the fucking reality? My Christ, I'm even teaching your lovely gardener English so that he can obey your every fucking whim. You think I can't recognise your wild cries amongst a thousand bird songs, whilst I sit locked in my tower trying to write our *Lady C*… and you play out that very fantasy. Why the hell do you think I was writing that fucking… fucking… (*He's near to breaking down, fighting for breath*)

FRIEDA: Oh, my God. Lawrence. I had no idea that you knew, that –

LAWRENCE: Just take me for a cuckold and a fool. Or a dead man already. A man who can no longer rise with the dawn. No death bed resurrection on offer from this one. You're right. A joke. Lawrence of all men can no longer stand. Well, wheel on the standing-in man. Standing-up. Lying down. All the positions under the morning fucking golden sun!

FRIEDA: Oh. Oh. Now I see.

LAWRENCE: No. I'm the one who sees. That's all that's left to me. See even when my eyes are tight shut. See even when the rain blinds me.

FRIEDA: Oh, my love. Please. I'll never leave you. Believe me.

LAWRENCE: Just fuck off! Fuck off, will you? Just have mercy, just for once, and just let me be!

Silence. FRIEDA *eventually goes. And now the rain is torrential. It slashes through the trees.* LAWRENCE *looks on the verge of collapse. He's fighting for breath.*

LAWRENCE: Steady Bertie old boy. Just so hot. How can it be. It's not rain, it's steam. Steam rising off of me. How is that... My mind. Galloping, galloping. Sunstroke. That bloody horse has got to me. Thoroughly. I must not see. Off, everything off. Come on. (*As he fights with his clothes*) Shirt. Bloody buttons. Come on. Yes. Everything. Let the thorns rip me apart. Everything off. Yes. (*Pause*) Been here before. Birkin. *Women in Love.* He ran naked in the rain, in the wood, yes, my own work augurs my own destiny. A prophet to himself. Why should I know too much. (*Bitterly*) Women in love. Off. Off. Come on, heaven burst your bowels, piss down on me! Let me hear you hiss as you hit my burning.

Burning, so tired and yet… Oh, God, why hast thou forsaken me. (*Laughs*) Steady, Bert, laddie, dinna get a bit above theesen. There be many a prophet but only one like he. Yet I imagine. (*Sighing*) There, there, yes. Rain, bless you. Extinguish me. Naked. I write the naked truth. Not even the fig leaf. No need. (*In thicker accent*) Ma', ma', I swallowed that black bible that thee gi' to me… And black, black, black it is. And offereth up nowt but bugger all. Forgive thee me. I mun turn to stranger Gods.

He stands holding up his arms to the rain. A strange yearning cry pierces the air. It's a cheetah on heat.

LAWRENCE: What the hell is… This place, it is a jungle. Tyger. I'm burning. (*Pause*) I don't know where I am. Please. Am I anywhere near the sea?

The rain pours down. LAWRENCE hisses loudly under it. He crouches, coughing, in pain on the edge of the pool. Eventually –

LAWRENCE: I want to live. I want to live. (*Rises*) It's too dark.

Fade to black. Fade up music –

Scene Two

The living room. Moulin du soleil.

MUSIC: Paris "musette", playing on a gramophone. (Emile Vacher's accordion piece – Reine De Musette).

Shadowy. The curved walls covered in images of the Sun God as well as photos, drawings, paintings of the Parisian in-crowd – Hart Crane, Joyce, Stein etc. A combination of the bohemian and the oriental mystical — carpets, cushions. A rough, traditional dining table. Looks like a room for parties, orgies and the occasional smoke. Which is what it is.

FRIEDA and CARESSE are painting portraits on Easter Eggs. HARRY is now changed into his clean whites. He stands by the door looking out. Frieda is humming away. Eventually —

HARRY: Should we not at least send out a search party?

FRIEDA: He would not want that.

HARRY: Ye', but it's one hell of a big domain here. He could easily be lost.

FRIEDA: My husband has been lost many times. That is part of the nature of his journey.

HARRY: (*Pause*) A little rain. The sun will break through. It's just taking its time. I'm really rather concerned that Lawrence might —

FRIEDA: Please you must not worry about him. He would not want that. It is only a little rain. The English are born water proof. So…

HARRY: It's just he's our guest, and I want him to be… I dunno, happy, I guess.

FRIEDA: That is kind. But sometimes you must know a man needs to rage. My husband says we never lose our demons, we simply have to wrestle them to the ground and make them work for us. Only priests claim success in chasing demons away.

HARRY: And they lie.

FRIEDA: I think so too.

CARESSE: More champagne, Harry?

HARRY: Sorry. Of course. Frieda, encore de champagne?

FRIEDA: The bubbles go straight to my nose. Why not?

He pops the cork and pours out the wine.

FRIEDA: Now. What colour must I paint my true love's eyes?

CARESSE: That's easy. Iridescent blue.

FRIEDA: (*Enigmatically*) Perhaps.

CARESSE: How could you forget?

FRIEDA: That's true.

She sighs, and drinks it down in one. HARRY fills her glass. She smiles up at him. LAWRENCE enters. He has managed to throw on a few clothes. FRIEDA doesn't look at him. Silence. He's strangely calm.

LAWRENCE: (*As he enters*) It's raining. (*Mildly*) Rather pleasant actually.

HARRY: You must get out of those wet clothes.

LAWRENCE: Don't worry about me. I'll just sit by the fire and steam gently.

CARESSE: Frieda has laid out others here for you. And here. There are hot towels.

LAWRENCE: Oh, yes. Towels. Thank you.

CARESSE: You should bathe.

HARRY: I'm afraid we don't have your English tin bath.

LAWRENCE: No need. I'm not black. Glittering with coal dust. The rain has washed me pure and clean.

HARRY: Do you feel absolved?

LAWRENCE: I'm not a Catholic. I look to no God to blame or redeem me. I am my sole authority.

HARRY: Soul?

CARESSE: You've cut your face a little.

LAWRENCE: (*Lightly*) A tree tried to embrace me.

FRIEDA: I hope you let it down gently.

LAWRENCE: (*Sharply*) What does that mean?

FRIEDA: Just a joke, Lorenzo.

He may seem calm but he's not in the mood for jokes.

CARESSE: (*Quickly*) Would you care to paint your Easter egg, Lawrence?

LAWRENCE: What?

HARRY: We are making our lover's portraits.

CARESSE: (*To* LAWRENCE: *smiling*) Well, actually I'm doing you.

HARRY: Why?

FRIEDA: Someone with a beard is so much easier to do.

CARESSE: I don't know if that's true. I'm afraid I've made your nose rather too big and the beard not burnished gold enough. (*Nervous*) Actually, I wondered, perhaps at some point might I do a sketch or two of you, and use them to make a proper bust. I'm not the most brilliant sculptress but –

HARRY: Truth is she's awfully good.

CARESSE: Well… would that, might that be possible?

LAWRENCE: If you desire.

FRIEDA: And if you can get him to sit still.

As LAWRENCE undresses and wraps himself in towels. Both CARESSE and HARRY politely look away. LAWRENCE seems not to care. HARRY pops open another bottle. LAWRENCE cries out.

HARRY: Glasses! Glasses!

CARESSE: You okay?

LAWRENCE: Just disappointed. Thought someone had shot the parrot.

HARRY: Champagne, Lawrence?

LAWRENCE: Not for me.

FRIEDA: Encore. Merci. (*Giggles*)

LAWRENCE: (*Flatly*) You're drunk.

Which happens to be quite true. And she will continue to drink fast and furious through the scene.

FRIEDA: Spoil sport.

She turns back to her egg. HARRY *hovers around* LAWRENCE. *He's now passing* LAWRENCE *items of clothing.*

HARRY: Lawrence, I really wanted to say to you earlier… something I've wanted to try to put into words for such a long time. Your masterpiece – *The Plumed Serpent.* Your re-discovery, your re-creation of the spirit of those lost Mexican gods of sex and death, Eros and Thanatos of a forgotten world, but still vibrant within our own forgotten souls, rising from the deep to challenge the suffocating death we call modern life. Now each of us must stand alone face to face with the serpents in all their fury and infinite vitality. Terrifying encounter, Lawrence, bloody, fearsome, but undeniable and ultimately hopeful. The only hope for life. (*Confidentially, the young boy surfacing in him*) Oh, Caresse will tell you, that book made me shake and shiver, and really changed my life, Lawrence. We read it aloud to each other on a boat on the Nile as we searched there for the same forgotten Gods only with different names – Isis, Osiris, their child Horus, and of course everywhere mighty Ra, the Sun God. It was a call to arms, to smash through this thin eggshell we call life, this pathetic shadow of reality, to search for something else, something truly, darkly, passionately alive. All my life I've tried to break through that shell. But *how*, this is what I can't quite…But you know, *you*… I just… I mean, *how*, how do we do it, once and for all? How finally do we utterly break through?

LAWRENCE: (*Apparently not paying attention: quietly*) May I see your egg now?

FRIEDA: Here.

LAWRENCE: The eyes should be brown.

FRIEDA: But it's meant to be you.

LAWRENCE: And he should have an Italian hat with a fine feather. Like a cock displaying his morning splendour.

FRIEDA: It is only a small egg, Lawrence. From a little hen.

LAWRENCE: (*Quietly*) How do we break through the eggshell, Harry? Well first, as you rightly say, we should turn to ancient Gods and myths for guidance, and you know what is the greatest song of all these?

HARRY: The Egyptian Book of the Dead?

LAWRENCE: Close. Now let me see if I remember. It's such perfect poetry: "Humpty Dumpty sat on the wall / Humpty Dumpty had a great fall" – (*As he drops the egg*) Whoops! Butter fingers. Sorry, my love.

FRIEDA: (*Unaffected*) Lorenzo is not a great admirer of other folk's art.

LAWRENCE: And why? Because they dare not go beyond the breaking. "All the king's horses and all the kings men / Couldn't put Humpty Together again." As if politics and armies could ever be the great healer. Let us not speak of Italy, Italy is but a pale shadow, full of men with silly feathers in their hats. Let us look at Germany.

FRIEDA: He loves to malign my Fatherland. Here, have another egg.

LAWRENCE: Germany. (*Drops the egg*) Whoops! Shattered by the war. And all the lunatic politicians can think to do is either glue bits back together again, or fall entranced before wild misreadings of Teutonic myths that give them a cheap, quick feel of superiority. *Übermensch*. One day we'll have to pay for such insanity as we'll have to pay for the craziness of Bolshevism and Americanism – the twin ideologies of madness.

FRIEDA: More eggs?

CARESSE: Thank the Lord our hens are such good layers.

LAWRENCE: Both are based on grab and greed. Of the two Americanism is the worst. Bolshevism only takes your home, but Americanism takes your very soul.

FRIEDA: Here they go.

LAWRENCE: Americanism.

FRIEDA: Bombs away.

He smashes another egg and turns to stare at HARRY.

HARRY: Right. Okay. I'm with the idea. Hand one to me.

CARESSE: How quickly men pick up bad habits. Here.

LAWRENCE: (*As* HARRY *smashes another egg*) What is that?

HARRY: I think you missed one, sir. Englishism. The disease of stagnation and rotting eggs. On the whole I consider it better to smash, than stagnate.

LAWRENCE: Why shop around for the best disease? They are only differing facets of the same dead soul of the modern world. We artists must go beyond that.

HARRY: Sure, but that's my question, how, how do we go beyond?

LAWRENCE: What is the next verse of Humpty Dumpty?

HARRY: I was not aware there was one.

LAWRENCE: Don't you feel there must be? Lost somewhere in the mist of history. Should we not at least try to find it, and if it does not exist yet, then bring it into being? All our endeavour as artists must be in search of that next verse, the verse that will free old Humpty Dumpty, that will truly put him back together again. And the truth lies in the shattered shards, in what we repress, that verse we have lost, that we dare not hear, but that we secretly long to speak. The darkness must be faced, the forbidden must be voiced. The answer takes heart but is to me quite clear. Humpty's resurrection is here, it is our Lady.

HARRY: (*Confused*) Our Lady? Mary?

LAWRENCE: Lady Chatterley. The missing verse. The book the world is dying to read, to burn, or both. The book to save the world. And it needs to save me too. The bitter irony is that I, the creator, earn nothing from it, I could die of starvation whilst in the States there are a dozen pirated versions, and the latest is the English threaten to ban my book there completely. Such is the battle, that is fine, I understand, but all I ask is enough resources to go on with my essential task of searching for the next verse. (*Exhausted for a moment*) And the next verse. (*Sighs*) Frieda and I were talking. When I met her at the *Gare du Nord*. We were saying how beautiful was your edition of "Sun". The most exquisite volume of any of my work. It made me weep. And it set a thought running. I have an idea to make us all a fortune. And buy me some space to breath. (*Smiling*) An expensive, deluxe, subscribers only connoisseurs' edition.

HARRY: Of what?

LAWRENCE: (*Excited*) Of my Lady Chatterley. When they banned Sir Richard Burton's translation of *The Arabian Nights* as outright pornography, all he did was change the spelling of cunt from c.u.n.t. to c.o.y.n.t.e. and bound the volume in leather and charged ten times as much as a subscriber edition. He made a fortune over night. And to gild our lily, they're opening an exhibition of my paintings in London, and we could add a number of those prints to this special edition. The images more than fit the tale — the dark mix of passion and paganism. Transgressive word and image savagely conjoined, and bound in perfect harmony. An irresistible work of art. What do you think? Perfect for Black Sun Press!

HARRY: (*Eventually*) Ah. Well. Yes. (*Shakes his head*) I'm terribly sorry, Lawrence, I fear we are unable to help you there.

LAWRENCE: Why not?

HARRY: Well, to be absolutely candid, Caresse and I we didn't really... Caresse!

CARESSE: No, Harry, not me. I can't.

HARRY: Oh. Right then. So it's up to me. Okay, let's go, right. (*Sighs*) I'm afraid that I, that we, we are rather of the opinion that perhaps Lady Chatterley lies somewhat beneath you. If you will forgive the rather obvious and unfortunate image.

LAWRENCE: Beneath me?

HARRY: I'm afraid we both have to be totally frank, we... well... (*Deep Breath*) we found it a trifle obscene.

LAWRENCE: A trifle obscene? Just a trifle?

FRIEDA: Lorenzo, stay calm.

HARRY: We're friends aren't we, please, I mean, I think, well, you wouldn't want us lying to you, we obviously so passionately admire your other work but this particular piece, it's, oh, God, we just feel it's not worthy of you, this rather obvious projection of yourself as some dark phallic force, with garlands crowning your priapic centre piece, well, frankly it all just looks a trifle, yes a trifle embarrassing and –

LAWRENCE: Embarrassing? For who?

HARRY: Well, for… look I'm sorry, it just seems to lack the presence of your normal magnificent imagination.

LAWRENCE: To lack my….

HARRY: Sorry, it just reads like a rather… well, a piece of wish-fulfilment.

   LAWRENCE *for once is speechless.*

FRIEDA: (*Sharply*) But you are quite wrong. You misread it. I'm not surprised you do. I think I myself I misread it too. But then I didn't know what Lorenzo knew, what this man was going through. Did not know until today.

CARESSE: Know what?

FRIEDA: (*Pauses then*) Ja, that is a work of the most immense imagination. And also, I must say, now that I see, one of superhuman courage and compassion. I don't believe there is another book or another writer anywhere who dares to go so far.

HARRY: I'd love to see that but… how is that?

FRIEDA: I'm so stupid. I thought certain things were hidden, and only now to see the pain, the pain it means to you, and how with such grace and courage you… oh Lorenzo, now I see.

CARESSE: See what?

LAWRENCE: Frieda, you are drunk. Sit down now.

FRIEDA: I will fight for you until my dying breath.

LAWRENCE: (*Quietly*) Nobody's fighting.

FRIEDA: Your mistake, Harry, Caresse, with the book, with the man, it's like mine. You think Lorenzo is the game-keeper, Mellors, the working-man, the – what you say – the priapic force, but no, no, Lorenzo is not Mellors. Mellors is not he. If Lorenzo is anyone in this work, and of course he is, he is her husband, Sir Clifford.

LAWRENCE: Take no heed. The woman's talking nonsense. Sir Clifford! A thorough-bred? Me? (*Tries to laugh*)

FRIEDA: (*To* HARRY *and* CARESSE) Can you not see the affinity?

LAWRENCE: Ridiculous. He's wounded in the war, I was not even in it.

FRIEDA: He's impotent.

LAWRENCE: A war wound. The man has a war wound. What's that to me? Woman's raving, leave her be.

FRIEDA: But Clifford, Lorenzo, this man you create, he is so generous. In his deepest heart against all his rage that's what he wants to be. And for that he must let his wife be free. You know this man, Sir Clifford, he is the true priest of love. He knows that I, that she, has needs.

Act One

CARESSE: Lady Chatterley? She's you?

FRIEDA: Yes, of course, well she is me, that's no question, never can be about this, but we speak now of his imagination, now he penetrates so deep in me. He can't help it. It is his genius, his hell. And yet in all that pain he does not judge. As much as it hurts.

LAWRENCE: Ravings, ravings, ravings. Any chance of tea?

CARESSE: Then who is this Mellors?

FRIEDA: Does not matter. What matters is he writes of him who cuckolds him with such compassion.

HARRY: But who is he?

FRIEDA: (*Eventually*) I've never said this before, my love. Because I didn't understand, didn't know how much you … until you told me that you knew. Didn't all this time really see the real greatness of you. You do pay in blood. You really do. *Danke, mein Liebster. Danke.*

Silence. LAWRENCE *remains quite still. The Jazz number comes to an end, and there is simply the sound of the record going round and round. Eventually –*

CARESSE: Dance? Let's dance, Frieda.

FRIEDA: Lawrence hates to dance.

CARESSE: Then dance with me.

She puts on Bessie Smith's "Empty Bed Blues".

FRIEDA: Oh, it is my favourite. I love this. I play it all the time. (*As she dances, joining in the song*) "I woke up this morning with an awful aching head, /I woke up this morning with an awful aching head…" I love this. "My new man had left me/ Just a room and an empty bed."

HARRY: (*Quietly*) Lawrence? Is this true? Is your wife correct?

LAWRENCE *doesn't seem to hear, preoccupied with gazing down at his hands.*

FRIEDA: "Bought me a coffee-grinder/Got the best I could find / Thought he could grind my coffee / 'Cos he had a brand new grind." Come on, Harry. Don't just sit there and stagnate. Harry, Harry, please. Don't leave the ladies lonely. Come grind the coffee. (*Laughs*)

Gaining no response from LAWRENCE, HARRY *finally nods, and decides to party.*

FRIEDA: (*Pause as he rises to join them*) Yes. Good man. *Das ist recht.* (*Laughs*)

CARESSE: "He's a deep sea diver / With a stroke that can't go wrong / He can touch the bottom / And his wind holds out so long…".

FRIEDA *and* CARESSE *(singing together as they share out movements with* HARRY): "He knows how to thrill me / And he thrills me night and day." *(Repeat)* "He's got a new way of loving, / Almost takes my breath away."

The dancing continues, with the three of them increasingly playing up the comic/erotic. In polite circles this would be called suggestive — here it may potentially be even more than that. As HARRY *and* FRIEDA *get into the Black Bottom mode — the blues rave dance of the time.*

CARESSE: "He's got that sweet something, / I told my girlfriend Lou, /For the way she's drinking, /she must have gone and tried him, too…"

LAWRENCE *seems in a world apart.*

ALL: "When my bed gets empty /Makes me feel awful mean and blue". *(Repeat)* "My springs are getting rusty / Sleeping single like I do…".

Finally, he rises − All three as they spin turn round and reach out to invite him in. Instead, he moves to the phonogram, takes off the record, studies it, and turns to face FRIEDA. *A beat. Then he smashes it over her head.* FRIEDA *cries out, but does not move.*

HARRY: Lawrence, what the hell are you doing?

CARESSE: My God. Frieda, has he cut your head?

FRIEDA: (*Vehemently*). *Arschloch! Macht sie dich wirklich so wild mit ihrer verflixten Kaffeemühle? Willst du ficken? Pech, Liebster! Hast nicht das Zeug dazu, meine ich.*[1]

Silence.

LAWRENCE: Good night.

He leaves the room. FRIEDA*'s breathing slowly settles down.*

FRIEDA: Do either of you speak German?

HARRY: No.

FRIEDA: *Das ist gut.*

---

[1] Asshole! Is she driving you crazy with her damned coffee grinder? You want to fuck? Too sad, sweetheart. I think you are a long way from being up to that.

CARESSE: Let me at least look at you.

FRIEDA: *Es geht mir gut.* (*Lightly*) *Guten Tag.* Sweet dreams.

   FRIEDA *goes after* LAWRENCE. CARESSE *kneels to pick up the broken pieces.*

CARESSE: I never really cared for this record myself. It has that terrible curse of the popular song. Truth.

She rises, and turns to HARRY

CARESSE: (*With no apparent trace of accusation*) Where were you last night, Harry? I thought that, after the opera, you were just popping in to see Joyce. Don't tell me he kept reading you "Work in Progress" all night?

As HARRY *settles at the table, and produces his magic box – his opium pipes and the heating lamp. (*HARRY*'s charm is he can move effortlessly from young boy comedy to Rimbaud mysticism – in short a classic bi-polar depressive. He's drugged and drunk.) As he lights the lamp –*

HARRY: No, just a sentence or two – (*Grins*) that took three hours, then he picked my pockets and propelled me out onto la rue. 'Twas from here, or perhaps at *Les Deux Magots,* pernod after pernod, I must have fallen into bad company, or good, depending on your point of view. Hemingway and Crane were there measuring penis size, not by any means all clear, not the size, the memory. Next I really recall I came round on the soft couches of our dream-makers from old Peking, with her Ladyship by my side.

CARESSE: (*Lightly*) That bitch Claudia.

HARRY: (*Equally mildly*) You know I can't resist her. She reminds me so of you.

CARESSE: Except she's blonde, and I'm brunette, has brown eyes whilst mine are blue. Oh ye', and she's a Countess and I'm a Brooklyn shop-girl.

HARRY: Minor details.

CARESSE: You've never let them bother you. So you two went on a white horse ride?

HARRY: We flew. Those Chinese. They have powerful, powerful stuff. I kind of recall writing the perfect end for 'Kubla Khan' but there you go, never a pen when you need one.

CARESSE: And… with the countess? Did you get the full ride?

HARRY: Well I might have fallen off. (*Grins*) I certainly got a little thrown about when her driver hit the train. Perhaps I should not have proffered him the flask but it was quite chilly.

CARESSE: And was her Highness damaged?

HARRY: No, she was fine and dandy. What's with this inquisition? Did your gentleman caller not turn up for tea?

CARESSE: I chose rather to read a book.

HARRY: Is that in reality what you wanted to do?

CARESSE: In reality? What is that, Harry? I don't know. If only my desires were clear to me.

HARRY: You desire to be desired.

CARESSE: That's a lazy route.

HARRY: Hm. I rather think it takes a certain courage.

CARESSE: To accept that? Or to refuse it?

HARRY: I love you.

CARESSE: Sure I know, but what does it mean, Harry, what is inside that golden box called love that you proffer to me? What comes flying out when I open up the lid? And is it the self-same present as that I proffer you?

HARRY: I believe it to be.

CARESSE: That's convenient. (*Pause*) So what exactly is this gift of love, Harry?

HARRY: Freedom.

CARESSE: Freedom from what?

HARRY: From possession, jealousy, from feeling another's soul or fearing that even your own can be owned. Ownership — that's not what love is — that's its shadow, the canker in the rose.

CARESSE: But does it have to be so hard?

HARRY: Of course. Come on, we've talked of this a thousand times, the entire, sunless, dead world is against us. We have to fight for it. Not simply dream about it, or merely write about it, whilst still continue to lie down with the lie. No, we must live it, live it. Live no longer in the shade, huddled no more in the cave, but walk out naked into the full fury of the mid-day sun. That's the difference between us.

CARESSE: Us?

HARRY: Lawrence and us. For him, for all his talent, all his words, his sun is merely a trick of the light, a tantalising turn of the line. I tell you, it's not real gold glinting in his beard, but the merest stain of muddy clay. And yet he speaks of everything as though he is God giving us the key.

CARESSE: He doesn't claim to be a God, Harry.

HARRY: He certainly claims the Holy Ghost fires his tongue, though. And perhaps in the past it did, but what happens when the spirit deserts him? Look at the filth he spouts forth now. Macabre fantasies of himself as a gamekeeper mounting a quivering Frieda, black hairs between her breasts. Imagine. Obsessed by fascination and shame.

CARESSE: According to Frieda, it's not himself he is imagining.

HARRY: Well, how pathetic can it be to imagine your wife making love with another man?

CARESSE: But of course you don't need to imagine.

HARRY: Because we dare to face whatever – together. No secrets. No shadows. We find a fear we look it straight in the eye in reality. We are not scared to truly risk. All he is is imagining and no action. Hasn't even the balls to live according to his own vision. You see, he can't face the final fact – to truly break through, to come through into the sun, one first has to meet death face to face.

Silence.

CARESSE: And you can.

HARRY: I have no fear of death.

CARESSE: (*Eventually*) Is that because you think you are dead already?

A beat, hardly a flicker. HARRY stands up. The opium is now bubbling away.

CARESSE: Don't turn away, please.

HARRY: (*Evenly*) Just want to change the tune.

He puts on a haunting, scratched and badly recorded, Arabic record — a Sufi (dervish) piece from Egypt. (Al' asfur sung by Sheik Ahmad Barrayn.) Initially the dervish solo instrument — the Ney. He picks up a pipe, and slowly begins to sway to the music.

HARRY: Time perhaps to ride the white horse, and perhaps the dance of the seven veils?

He holds out his pipe to her.

CARESSE: I don't know, Harry. I don't know if I want to play.

HARRY is not offended. He smiles. As the vocals begin he mimes them. He sways gently in front of her, slowly spinning like a spaced-out dervish. CARESSE watches him.

As the drums join in, the lights fade —

End of Act One

Act Two

Scene One

The Pool.

The following morning − Easter Sunday. Daybreak. LAWRENCE sits, his notebook on his knee. He is a shadow amongst shadows. He does not move. A rare silence.

And then − a cockerel crows thrice. A stirring into life. A whisper through the trees. LAWRENCE sighs.

LAWRENCE: Perfect. Thank you. (*Lightly: Starts to read*) And the cock crows thrice. Doesn't it just? "And at the same time, at the same hour before dawn, on the same morning, a man awoke from a long sleep in which he was tied up. He woke numb and cold, inside a hole in the rock." What kind of hole, Lawrence? Man-made? Hollowed, chiselled? "a carved hole in the rock". A womb for the man who died. And? "Through all the long sleep his body had been full of hurt, and it was still full of hurt."

A sleepy FRIEDA appears in her multi-flowered silk dressing-gown. The vibrancy of its colours alone would wake up Rip Van Winkle.

FRIEDA: Lorenzo. Oh. I wake and you are not… what are you doing?

LAWRENCE: What do I ever do, my dear? Go back to bed. (*Mumbling*) Banded with cold bands…

FRIEDA: We need to talk.

LAWRENCE: Has not enough been said?

FRIEDA: I'm stupid, stupid, stupid, you know that. My mouth runs away with me. If they race me at Chantilly I'll beat even Harry's thoroughbred. Come on, please, Lorenzo, I apologise, I am so sorry.

LAWRENCE: What could you possibly have to apologise for, my love? For being a prophetess, for seeing more deeply into the dark recess of my soul than I see myself? Because of course I am blind, the eyeless artist, thrashing around in the pitch of caves, having lost my way. Banded and bandaged together. Apologise, no, bless you, my lady of the lamp, for casting the light of understanding on my creative power, the only power I now possess, I have no others as a mere man to boast of, and I need you to proclaim unto the entire world the meaning of what I write, why I write, how bound in some wheel-chair of the mind the passion no longer flames my loins, but my imagination still flies − how brave and noble of your husband to imagine others between your thighs.

He is suddenly exhausted.

FRIEDA: My love.

LAWRENCE: Do you know what happens to me , when you murmur his name as you sleep, when he pierces you in your dream? Do you know the knife it takes to me? To be denied in my own bed.

FRIEDA: I don't deny, I'd never deny my love for you.

LAWRENCE: Oh, so, what, you call out my name when you come with him? You don't cry out 'Angelo, *mein lieber* Angelo', no, no, but 'Lorenzo', of course, yes, how sweet, so kind, so well bred! (*Sharply*) No, don't try to fob me off he's just some shadow replacement, last minute substitute for tennis hardly a master of the racquet but at least the exercise is good. Or that you never look him in the eye, it's simply a question of dogs squatting on haunches in the sun, a moment's cough and all is done. Don't you dare. I've heard you, seen you, seen every moment from first glance, first touch, gesture, kiss, cry, every twisting combination of position. Of course you know this, as you say, as you told the world, I've even sat for hours making dainty daisy chains to wrap around his fucking cock. Oh, how tired I am of that word cock, that's all I seem to think of, how many times do you cry before the cock crows thrice? I hate this story. May I never hear the word cock or fuck or cunt again for all my life!

He throws his papers towards the pool.

FRIEDA: Missed.

LAWRENCE: I wasn't aiming at you. (*Exhausted*) Some other ghost who won't stay dead.

Silence. FRIEDA *sighs.*

FRIEDA: If it consoles you, I've never woven daisies around his…

LAWRENCE: (*Exhausted*) No, I know. They were Bavarian gentians.

Silence.

FRIEDA: Yes.

LAWRENCE: (*Softly*) You are stupid.

FRIEDA: I said that first.

She begins to pick up the manuscript.

FRIEDA: Lorenzo. I know this hurts, but as we speak of this now. You know what I need to say.

LAWRENCE: (*Quietly*) I can't go back to Italy, Frieda. I simply can't.

FRIEDA: Sir Clifford could live with it.

LAWRENCE: I can make him live with anything. Because he is not real. (*Pause*) But I on the other hand… (*Sighs*) The best I can do, Frieda, is… Every heart has a right to its own secrets. I do not ask. Will not. And I'll struggle not to imagine.

He kneels with difficulty to help pick up the papers. They are close together. He gazes at a page, then —

LAWRENCE: (*Pause*) What I can't face…. (*Shakes his head*) I don't want to see your future without me mapped out in front of me. It only makes me impotent and angry. But it doesn't mean I don't wish you a future. A future beyond me. I do. Desperately.

FRIEDA: I will not leave you. I love you, Lorenzo. And I know you love me.

LAWRENCE: (*Pauses*) That is no secret, Frieda. But does it help either of us?

FRIEDA: What can I do, *hein*? Just tell me.

LAWRENCE: (*Exhausted*) Just let me write.

She rises, hands him the manuscript, a beat, a stillness as he reaches out for them. They almost touch.

LAWRENCE: Frieda.

He sees CARESSE appear behind her. CARESSE is the only one who seems to have dressed for the day.

CARESSE: Hi. Oh, don't mean to disturb. I… just seem to

have lost everybody.

LAWRENCE: Happy Easter.

He turns to walk away.

CARESSE: Please don't go.

LAWRENCE: (*Lightly*) I need to go further into the heart of darkness.

He goes.

CARESSE: Bad timing?

FRIEDA: When he quotes another writer, one always must be careful. Although Conrad is dead, so that is not quite so bad.

She smiles, and starts on her first cigarette. She beckons CARESSE to sit by her.

CARESSE: I am sorry.

FRIEDA: It is not you anyway, it is me who must say sorry – for last night. Bubbles are always troubles for me. And I apologise also for Lorenzo. He would apologise himself but he's not yet found the word in his dictionary. I will mark and underline for him. It's... he feels so passionate about his Lady. Full of words that must be spoken that are not even in the dictionary. That is the whole point, you see. The book is a new world, with a new language. A language to make us free. You should really publish. (*Pauses*) No?

CARESSE: (*Evading*) There's really no need to apologise. We were just worried for you. That record must have really hurt.

FRIEDA: No. I once smashed a very big plate, soup plate,

tureen, right on top of his head. In Cornwall. It was the War. One does these things in war. It is the price of being his inspiration.

CARESSE: But how does he know all about you and… ? He writes so truthfully about women. Is it that you confess everything?

FRIEDA: No need for that. He can smell the truth on me. (*Pause: Smiles*) He has a wonderful nose. When you sculpt you remember this. Lorenzo could stand in your meadow and name every flower in the field from its fragrance. He smells love on me no matter how hard I scrub.

CARESSE: Sometimes…

FRIEDA: *Hein?*

CARESSE: (*Uncertain*) Sometimes – often – no, maybe always –

FRIEDA: Yes?

CARESSE: I also make love under another's perfume. Some other woman's, or even… In Egypt, on our honeymoon, Harry brought a boy to bed. He carried him in wrapped in a rug like Cleopatra. Rolled him out unto my feet. His musk lingered on our love until we were back in Paris, and the waves of some girl's Attar of Roses swept it away. I know Harry by his other loves. He offers up his conquests as proudly as a cat leaving the gift of mouse upon your pillow. He plays with them and brings them home to share, in the flesh or in the perfumed shadow. (*Pause*) I just wish sometimes –

FRIEDA: What?

CARESSE: That I could just smell him. But without *le parfum des autres*, I would never find him in the dark. (*Pause*) He says that I am his inspiration.

She shakes her head, unsure. Silence.

CARESSE: Do I shock you?

FRIEDA *simply looks at her, smiling.*

CARESSE: And you… you still remain his sole source of inspiration?

FRIEDA: Yes of course. But not, I'm afraid, his cure. My husband has consumption. He is dying. There. Said.

Silence.

CARESSE: (*Stunned*) Is there no hope?

FRIEDA: What? Of resurrection? You still clutch on to Christian myths? Well, why not, yes, of course, it is Easter. And the man yearns on life. Perhaps, but I am not the one to do the resurrecting. Who knows? You really think such a thing is possible?

CARESSE: (*Smiling*) Harry is constantly resurrected. It's almost a daily treat.

FRIEDA: And who brings him back to life again? You? Or some other? (*Pause*) I think perhaps if someone came, someone who knew, understood, and blew upon the ashes, perhaps my dying phoenix would take wing again. Perhaps…? What do you think? And perhaps such a thing might inspire this wonder woman too?

FRIEDA *gently touches her face.*

FRIEDA: Caresse. Such a beautiful name. Such a beautiful thing to be.

Silence. Then suddenly a chant breaks through the air – it's HARRY's own version of the Egyptian "Layalli" – the song to the sky (translated, the chant calls all to turn their faces to the sun). It seems to set off a similar desire in all the animals including the donkeys. FRIEDA freezes, then turns to stare at him. CARESSE is locked in her own thought as – LAWRENCE returns.

LAWRENCE: What on earth is that cacophony?

CARESSE: It's Harry, chanting to his sun-god for fine weather. He wants everything to be perfect for you.

LAWRENCE: Well, it doesn't seem to be working.

CARESSE: It had better.

FRIEDA: What happens if the sun does not break through?

CARESSE: Then it is very dark. For him.

LAWRENCE: And for you?

CARESSE: I try to keep a little candle lit.

LAWRENCE continues to watch her. She looks down under the heat of this study. HARRY's chant now turns to invocation echoing through the trees.

HARRY: (*Voice*) *I exchange eyes with the Mad Queen*
The mirror crashes against my face
And bursts into a thousand suns
I crash out the window
Naked widespread upon a Heliosaurus…

Act Two

LAWRENCE: A Heliosaurus?

CARESSE: Harry likes to play with words.

LAWRENCE: Or do they play with him?

HARRY: (*Voice*) *I uproot an obelisk and plunge*
  It into the ink-pot of the
  Black Sea

FRIEDA: Where? Where is he? I cannot see.

CARESSE: Look. There. Perched as in a nest on the top of the
  tower.

FRIEDA: *Mein Gott.* Lorenzo, look. All in white. Like an angel.

HARRY: (*Voice*) *I write the word SUN*
  Across the dreary palimpsest
  Of the world

LAWRENCE: (*Glancing up*) Or an embalm-ed corpse.

FRIEDA: Yes, perhaps, incanting to push the heavy rock aside.
  It is Easter.

LAWRENCE: What rock?

FRIEDA: The grey, grey sky. To reveal the light to the world.

LAWRENCE: So now *he* is Christ. Make up your mind.

HARRY: (*Voice*) *I am the harbinger of a new world SUN*
  I bring the seed of a New Copulation

LAWRENCE: What was wrong with the old copulation?

CARESSE: (*Smiling*) I rather thought you would know that.

HARRY: (*Voice*) *I proclaim the Mad Queen!*

   LAWRENCE *is staring at* CARESSE.

CARESSE: What do you think?

LAWRENCE: Of what?

CARESSE: Harry's poetry.

LAWRENCE: Is this my moment for revenge?

CARESSE: Is there need for that?

HARRY: (*Voice*) *Look Lawrence. I'm breaking through!*

FRIEDA: How does he get up there in the first place?

LAWRENCE: He flies. All angels fly. If rather pointlessly to my mind.

CARESSE: But the real trick is how does he get down.

   HARRY *cries out not unlike the cheetah on heat.*

FRIEDA: Oh, *Mein Gott,* no. how is … it's true. Look. (*Gasps*) He really can fly. He's sailing through the sky. Is this for real?

CARESSE: Hidden ropes and wires.

LAWRENCE: Endless imitation.

   FRIEDA *whoops as* HARRY *enters. He wears a white linen Egyptian robe. Arms outstretched.*

HARRY: (*Quietly*) *And Lo! Behold! I am manifest.*

He bows quietly, pleased with his little trick. FRIEDA *is more impressed than* LAWRENCE.

FRIEDA: Amazing, my young God. Truly. Truly. An Angelo.

LAWRENCE: Angelo?

HARRY: (*Grinning*) At last. Some-one recognises the real me.

LAWRENCE: What need have we for Angelos?

FRIEDA: *Wunderbar.* How do you do this flying? It was like something from a Douglas Fairbanks film. He had better watch his shadow, *hein?*

HARRY: Actually it was the great man himself who taught me how to do it. He rigged up all the ropes for me.

FRIEDA: (*Stunned*) Douglas Fairbanks, he has been here? *Mein Gott!* Now I am truly impressed. I saw his new film *The Iron Mask* in Baden Baden. What a man. So charming, but also so… noble. We loved it.

LAWRENCE: (*Sharply*) *We* didn't see it.

FRIEDA: (*Quickly*) Lorenzo was not there, but he hates cinema anyway.

LAWRENCE: All the famous people *we* meet and you have to drool over some muscle-bound actor.

HARRY: Not just some actor, surely? Probably the greatest film actor of our generation.

LAWRENCE: Film. The grey imitation of life. I'd rather go to a *séance*. At least there you get the chance to answer the dead back.

FRIEDA: (*Lightly*) He must always answer back. Often before he has even heard the question.

LAWRENCE: Our task as artists is to *discover* the question. That sometimes means sweeping aside a thousand fake answers.

HARRY: Like what?

LAWRENCE: Like that the sun will shine at our bidding.

FRIEDA: (*A beat*) But it has, Lorenzo. It's beginning to break through now, look, look at the light now, oh it reminds me so of Italy.

LAWRENCE: (*Sharply*) It is utterly different, the light here. Utterly!

CARESSE: (*Quickly*) So what shall we all do today? Now the sun looks to be kind to us.

HARRY: I rather thought to take Lawrence flying with me. I wanted to show you the heart of the sun.

LAWRENCE: I'm too old to swing on ropes like Peter Pan. I'll leave that to those who never grew up.

CARESSE: No, no, Harry has a plane, Lawrence.

FRIEDA: Lorenzo gets sick on boats, dear. I don't think a plane's a good idea. But perhaps for me.

HARRY: (*Hurt*) What do you mean – never grew up?

LAWRENCE: I don't get sick on boats. I just hate the obsession with speed, the false throb of the engines, giving you some pale imitation of sexual ecstasy. That's all the boys want with their fast cars, and boats, and soaring planes.

HARRY: Oh, I see, that's why you think the little boy flies. (*Struggling to restrain himself*) Is that it, you believe that the rest of us can be nothing but pale imitation. It's not fair, Lawrence. It's not right. I mean there are those of us who can still rise up for the real thing. We at least, unlike some, are ready and primed and up for action. Who is imitating here, Lawrence? Words can throb upon a page but are they not still only the tool of the voyeur of life?

LAWRENCE: (*A beat*) Voyeur, what, what did you say?

CARESSE: Harry! Harry! He didn't mean anything about… it wasn't…

LAWRENCE: What did you say?

HARRY: (*Trying to appease*) Sorry, I… my mouth… I'm warned often … just meant that… I wasn't in any −

LAWRENCE: You are so sure in your potency. So go on, with your endless parroting of the words gold and sun, as though the mere repetition of a mock litany will really usher in the New Dawn.

FRIEDA: Let us all please −

HARRY: All I'm saying is, come on, you can't just be the only one mature enough to speak of life and death?

LAWRENCE: What do you know of death? (*Pause*) I face it in every breath. Your generation flirts with it through the bars, as though you had it locked up with the rest of your private menagerie.

HARRY: I face the dark as much as any man.

LAWRENCE: You play with your planes, and drugs and women, it's all a game – you'll meet death as lost as anyone. Your art is only gold painted egg shells. You are a hollow Easter, for all your talk of rebirth.

HARRY: Well, at least the artists of my generation had the guts not to shirk the war like one or two of yours.

CARESSE: Oh, no, Harry!

LAWRENCE: No, you ran to it, like lemmings dreaming on the thrill of death. More fool you in hurtling to the kill.

HARRY: We didn't go to kill. We went to heal. I drove an ambulance.

LAWRENCE: Don't give me that. You came to play at cowboys on the open range.

HARRY: At least I didn't stand by, whining impotently.

CARESSE: Shut up, Harry!

LAWRENCE: (*Pauses*) Whining. Impotently.

HARRY: Sorry, but this man has no right to… good men died and he….

CARESSE: Wait! Wait. Just take breath. And tell him. Tell him the truth of what it was like for you. (*Eventually*) Harry was just turned eighteen, he volunteered. He and his best friend Michael they were kids, fresh out of high-school.

Act Two

HARRY: This is stupid.

CARESSE: They didn't want to kill anyone. Both bright young boys. Both saw the war's insanity. They just wanted to save lives. Mick was blown to bits by Harry's side in their ambulance. There was no resurrection then.

HARRY: Caresse.

CARESSE: No, I'm going to say it. Harry walked away unmarked. But I'm not sure that he actually survived. Harry, you see, Lawrence, Harry really thinks he's dead already. He thinks he is a ghost, dreaming on life.

HARRY: This is just crazy.

CARESSE: Yes, it is. Harry listen to me. (*Carefully*) You didn't die in that ambulance at Verdun. Okay, Mickey, your best friend did, that's true, he was blown to smithereens, his body and his blood came raining down on you. You practically breathed the man you loved. Please. Please. I'm sorry, I know we do not talk of this… but… all you do… the drugs, sex, the chanting to forgotten Gods, listen to me Harry, please, you are not dead, there's no need to fight so hard for resurrection into life. You are not dead. Believe me. I've held you. I know the difference between a corpse and living flesh.

HARRY: What are you raving on about? You sound like him. I've never said I was dead. I simply face death head on. That's the way to seize life by the throat.

CARESSE: Don't be angry.

HARRY: I'm not angry.

CARESSE: I'm just scared, Harry.

HARRY: Of what?

Silence. LAWRENCE studies HARRY as he once looked at his wife. HARRY turns away shyly.

FRIEDA: Lorenzo.

LAWRENCE: (*Quietly*) I am fine, thank you. (*Eventually*) Harry. I… (*With great difficulty*) I would like to…. (*Sighs*)

FRIEDA: The word is apologise.

CARESSE: And Harry too.

HARRY: (*Eagerly*) Oh, yes, I do. Most sincerely.

LAWRENCE: I in turn… (*Coughs*) You talk of Egyptian Gods. Isis. Osiris. Ra. And I wonder if… I am working on a new story. It's called the Escaped Cock, God knows they're probably ban it for the title alone. But perhaps. If Our Lady does not for whatever reason… I… er… perhaps this piece might interest. It's a kind of Easter story. About Jesus. After his resurrection. Dickens did so well out of Christmas, and so I thought why not try the same with Easter. (*Shrugs, almost a laugh*)

CARESSE: Please. Tell us. Please.

LAWRENCE *looks at* HARRY.

HARRY: Please.

LAWRENCE: (*Evenly*) It begins at the end. The man is crucified. He dies. The cry of a crested cockerel wakes him back into life. But what life? His body is battered badly, but what of his soul? He rises and travels to the edge of the sea, where he meets a young woman, a temple virgin, a celebrant of an even more ancient spirituality, the votary of Isis, waiting for her God Osiris to return. And she sees in this man, whose tortured soul has been scattered to the four winds, the image of her own Lord waiting on her love to resurrect him fully and completely. At first, so tentative to the pain of touch is he, and so fearful to be trapped again in the terrible compulsion of love, that he denies her and her balm and all her blessing. *Noli Me Tangere* — do not touch me.

CARESSE: But her love finally heals him?

LAWRENCE: They, in a way, resurrect each other, for she, too, has travelled through a similar vale of death, but in a different way.

CARESSE: What way?

LAWRENCE: Daily death by boredom, shame, suppression and swallowed rage.

CARESSE: (*Smiling*) But now they live happily ever after and bear forth fruit? Like the new Adam and Eve, no longer scared to eat the apple. With little baby Horus bouncing on her knee. Isn't that how Dickens would have finished his Easter story?

LAWRENCE: Unquestionably.

HARRY: But how does Lawrence end it?

LAWRENCE: I have yet to answer that. All I know is at the moment he stands on the edge of the sea.

CARESSE: But why is there a need to go further? Haven't you resurrected Jesus at last by true love? Isn't that enough?

LAWRENCE: I haven't resurrected Jesus. I have simply cut

him free from the cord of faith around his neck that threatens to strangle us all. He does not survive the cross *because* he is Christ, but because he finally refuses the false myth of Divinity. The lie of easy resurrection and eternal salvation that is death for all of us in life. But that is different from meeting death itself.

CARESSE: So now he is a mere mortal, does he fear death? Is he running away from it?

HARRY: No. A true man must stand up to death and not wait for it to call the day. That should be our choice. Just as we have the divine right to choose the last rhyme of a poem, the final line of the tale, that brings completion, shape and meaning, so we must do the same with our lives. We can call the day, and meet it face to face. That's what Caresse and I have done.

LAWRENCE: You have chosen the day to die?

FRIEDA: I hope it's not this weekend. We are having so much fun.

CARESSE: September 3rd, 1944.

HARRY: (*Lightly*) You are invited to the party.

LAWRENCE: Why would you choose to die?

HARRY: Because it's the only really true choice one can make.

LAWRENCE: But you are playing death's game. Forget the poetry for one moment. There is no certain resurrection into a life where you can rise again refreshed. Death is the absence of life and is unforgiving and unforgivable.

CARESSE: (*Carefully*) Does death frighten you?

LAWRENCE: (*Pause*) Not every tale is an autobiography.
  Silence.

HARRY: So what would we all like to do?

FRIEDA: I want to catch a little sun. It has been so long.

HARRY: And perhaps risk a little swim.

CARESSE: Don't be silly, Harry. It will be freezing.

FRIEDA: In Baden Baden we had to break the ice.

LAWRENCE: (*Quietly*) We?

CROSBY: I'll get some towels. Just in case.

CARESSE: And the hamper. We can breakfast here.

CROSBY: And we'll sit and sip champagne and talk of poetry.

FRIEDA: And the resurrection of the phoenix.

She smiles at CARESSE *as they turn to leave. Silence. They seem almost shy of each other.* FRIEDA *moves a little, like a lizard searching for the sun, as it breaks through the foliage.* LAWRENCE *watches her. She turns to look at him. He does not this time turn away. The spell is broken by the distant sounds of a church bell.*

LAWRENCE: Easter Sunday. (*With heavy accent*) Eh little shirty Bertie lad, dust thou still recall to mind? Coun't forget. That were big day for all 'n 'us. Mam scrubbed us to bone for chapel, white collars so starched to 'eavenly stiffness, thou dare not turn thee 'ead for fear of slicing it off. We trooped in fine array, even me dad shone polished in the sickly sun. We had our little row, knew our place, God was in his Heaven and we were on his bench, lasses in home-made bonnets and lads in itchy britches. Aye, an' how lustily we belted out them old hymns. (*Relishing the word*) Lustily.

He begins merrily to sing the chorus of the old redemption hymn –
"VICTORY".

LAWRENCE: *Alleluia! Alleluia! Alleluia!*
The strife is o'er, the battle done;
The victory of life is won,
The song of triumph has begun.
Alleluia!
Hm. Strange what comfort a triple rhyme can be. The magic of the mystic number three. It leads us on but where the hell are we? (*Smiling*) See, there, I did it myself.

FRIEDA: And are you comforted?

LAWRENCE: The triple is a trick of doggerel. Satisfies but not for long. Like everything else, poetry must be freed from its own particular tyranny.

FRIEDA: What is your particular tyranny? Is it me?

LAWRENCE: Don't be silly. (*Pause*) Am I yours?

FRIEDA: I forbid you to think such a thing. Now I am a tyrant, you see.

He looks at her. She shivers. She moves to stand in the next patch of sun.

FRIEDA: I think they are so beautiful, don't you?

LAWRENCE: What?

FRIEDA: Our hosts.

LAWRENCE: I think they are lost like all their generation.

FRIEDA: Is that not part of their beauty?

LAWRENCE: (*Gently*) No depth. They are like the surface of this pool. It's merely the reflection of the sun that makes them glitter, the wind that gives them shape, not their own true breath of inspiration. All so delicate, yes, because imitation is such a fragile skin. Harry is wrong. Death is the end of a story that only others can tell. And then, of course, it's no longer your story.

FRIEDA: (*Simply*) I will be there for you always.

LAWRENCE: (*Gently*) You imagine you are answering something that I have asked?

Silence. CARESSE *and* HARRY *appear carrying hamper, sketch pad and towels.*

HARRY: *Voila, mes amis.* The survival kit.

CARESSE: This should keep us going for a little while. (*Smiles*) We really ought to have eggs but… well, I'm sure they will lay some more.

FRIEDA: Just make sure they are hard-boiled next time.

HARRY: And now − for one of the mysteries of the deep.

He finds a line and pulls up a bottle of champagne from the pond.

HARRY: Champagne! Caresse, glasses. The day of resurrection is upon us.

LAWRENCE: Aren't we going to wait for your old magician friend, Count Cagliostro? Isn't he supposed to be reborn here?

HARRY: Perhaps he's here already. He comes in many disguises.

LAWRENCE: (*Mildly*) You said that once before. It didn't make any sense then.

HARRY: This is not a place of sense, Lawrence. You above all must understand that. It's maybe beneath, maybe beyond, all that. Sense is only the reading of shadows. A blind man trying to understand a painting. Or a man with no taste who writes of champagne.

He pops the cork. CARESSE *and* FRIEDA *rush forward with glasses.*

HARRY: To Easter. For *tout le monde. Paques Heureux!*

FRIEDA: *Glückliches Ostern!*

CARESSE: Happy Easter!

LAWRENCE: (*Quietly*) Happy Easter.

He only sips his wine.

FRIEDA: This rebirth thing you speak off with the pool, does it only work for your mad magician friend?

HARRY: Well now we had better put it to the test. Let's go dive in and see into what new life you surface.

LAWRENCE: Not wise, Frieda.

A beat. She turns away and begins to loosen her dressing-gown.

HARRY: Come on, Lawrence, come and join us. Look! The sun is breaking through!

LAWRENCE: I fear it's not for me.

HARRY: Caresse?

CARESSE: I will stay here and sketch Lawrence. (*To* LAWRENCE) If I may?

LAWRENCE: Of course. Where would you like me? Should I sit beneath the willow tree?

LAWRENCE *sits on the bench. Upstage,* HARRY *laughs as he and* FRIEDA *start stripping off.*

HARRY: Last one in's a chicken. And must lay the eggs for lunch.

LAWRENCE: Frieda, you have no costume.

She doesn't seem to hear. CARESSE *now watches* LAWRENCE *intently. He becomes aware of this.*

LAWRENCE: What's the point? These Germans. They shed their clothes at a postcard of the sun. Put a bucket of water in front of them and they'll dive straight in.

CARESSE: The English are so different?

LAWRENCE: God, yes. When we come to water we're all too aware we hover on the brink of a new world, and one to be entered with due English propriety. So we build not boats but small houses on wheels, wherein we change, and then the houses are slowly slid into the shallow edge of the sea. But of course tethered tight by ropes to stop them escaping. I often dream of all those little English homes floating free towards the horizon. And that I am he who cut the ties.

FRIEDA: (*Triumphant: laughing*) Too slow!

She stands naked. LAWRENCE now looks at her. She notices. He looks away. She dives into the pool, and screams with the shock.

FRIEDA: *Wunderbar.* Bugger Baden Baden! (*Calling*) Come on, Harry! Chicken!

She clucks at him. He cock-a-doodle's back at her.

LAWRENCE: Cockadoodle dandy.

CARESSE: What?

LAWRENCE: Another song I hate.

He closes his eyes.

FRIEDA: (*Calling*) You'll never catch me!

HARRY: (*Laughing*) You've no chance.

He dives in. As they disappear out of sight, splashing and laughing, the sound fades away. CARESSE has begun to sketch. Time could have passed. Eventually —

CARESSE: (*Softly*) Lawrence? Are you asleep? Lawrence?

LAWRENCE: (*Lightly*) Oh, do you need my eyes open for your sketch? I rather imagined you'd leave them blank, as the ancient sculptors did. The blind prophet, unheeded Tiresias, but *not* your garrulous parrot kind.

CARESSE: Is that how you believe the world sees you?

LAWRENCE: (*Softly*) I no longer care, as long as it doesn't pester me with adoration. Or the sheer stupidity of imitation. Like Harry. Caught in the insane belief that by enacting what his artist heroes did, he'll somehow touch their inner vision. Baudelaire, Joyce, Whitman, me, who cares, he's a man who jumps from iceberg peak to peak, and believes he knows therefore the hidden depths. The sun does not illuminate his world. The boy is snow-blind. Ice without fire. If he stops hopping for just one minute, the frostbite of his soul will set in. And so he dare not stop. But one day soon, when tiredness hits… Then…

He looks directly at her.

CARESSE: (*Pause*) Is it compulsory for you to see into another's soul? It seems so un-English.

LAWRENCE: Let me close my eyes awhile. There's nothing I need to see.

CARESSE: They've swum out of sight anyway.

LAWRENCE: But not out of vision.

CARESSE: (*Pause*) Okay, you know I can't resist, Tiresias. What does that mean? What do you see?

LAWRENCE: No more than what is. Cagliostro's magic pool. Frieda, standing, water rippling round her hip. A dark shadow under the pool's thin skin, brushing her thigh. And lo! The young god breaks through, shaking the wet from off his hair. Give Harry a stick between his faultless teeth and he'd make the perfect golden retriever.

CARESSE: You don't mind that Frieda and he…. That even as we speak they might be… I rather thought for you it would be…

LAWRENCE: (*Pauses*) Is what they say of you true?

CARESSE: What do they say?

LAWRENCE: That you and your American friends circle your cars like covered wagons in the *Bois de Boulogne* and all go "loving" in the headlamps glare?

CARESSE: So you listen to gossip? I rather imagined you were above all that.

LAWRENCE: I'm above nothing. As time passes, I just slip further and further to one side. (*Pauses*) How do you feel about his other women?

CARESSE: (*Pauses*) Harry loves me. But marriage somewhat stripped me of the mystique of the veil for him. And when Harry sees a veil he feels honour bound to pull it aside.

LAWRENCE: You haven't answered my question.

CARESSE: (*Pauses*) I know that at heart whoever's veil he lifts, at the moment of ecstasy, it's my face he will see.

LAWRENCE: (*Softly*) How convenient for you. You save all that massive expenditure of energy, and still retain full possession. What a shit he is. At least when Frieda pants upon her private pleasure she has the decency to not imagine me. Put him on the pyre and burn the bugger!

CARESSE: Why is everything anger with you? I don't understand what you say. I've never really felt anger.

LAWRENCE: And yet you say you love?

CARESSE: What has anger to do with love?

LAWRENCE: (*Pauses: Quietly*) I've been angry all my life. A burning rage from poisoned lungs. And now most of all I rage against…

CARESSE: Who? Frieda? But she loves you so.

LAWRENCE: Not Frieda. (*Pause*) Death. That that threatens to rob me of everything. I don't want to hold life in the palm of my hand like some Victorian curate pinning down the beauty of a butterfly. I want to *be* life, with all its coarseness and delicate delight, I want to be the essence within everything, not to possess, but to enjoin, to unite, to be the very breath of inspiration and death aims to cheat me of that.

This sudden fury brings on a coughing fit. Eventually —

LAWRENCE: To be angry and tired. It may well be a deadly combination.

Silence. CARESSE *sighs, and stands.*

CARESSE: I think I'll join them in a swim.

LAWRENCE: Watch out for the *parfum* of Prussian pulchritude.

CARESSE: Your wife tells you everything?

LAWRENCE: As much as I want to hear.

She stands quietly for a moment, then starts to strip in front of him. LAWRENCE *looks down and closes his eyes.*

CARESSE: Don't close your eyes, Lawrence. Now you must look at me. Blast these buttons. Look at me!

LAWRENCE: (*Pause: Looking at her*) Am I under compulsion?

Is it mine or yours?

CARESSE: Don't deny me, Lawrence. Please. (*Struggling with her clothes*) Got it. There. That's better. Now.

LAWRENCE: Is this the Yankee doodle version of the Seven Veils?

CARESSE: If that would please. What do you think of this brassiere? I invented it, you know, really, truthfully, I did. I was a young girl, crazy, poor, wanting the end of whale bone stricture, wanting like you to breathe. My gift of inspiration. But I sold it, like you, too cheaply. (*As she takes it off*) Please, look at me. Please. (*Sighs*) Now these breasts, do you know they won the best breasts prize at last year's Arts Ball? And there was stiff competition. (*Laughs*) What do you think? Do they deserve an award? (*Now finally naked*) And what of this, Lawrence? What of this? Now you see the woman that is truly me. You can touch. You can kiss. You can caress. However, however you wish. (*Pause*) Do you not desire me?

LAWRENCE: (*Pause: Quietly*) Does not everyone? Isn't that just a tad boring?

CARESSE: Do you?

LAWRENCE: What does it matter?

CARESSE: It matters to me.

LAWRENCE: (*A beat*) "I am worn out / with the effort of trying to love people / and not succeeding."

CARESSE: Please, don't hide behind poetry.

LAWRENCE: No one has ever accused me of that before. Normally, they ask me to veil my naked words.

CARESSE: It's Caresse now who is naked beyond words. Lawrence, don't mock me, please. Could it not be…what if I am the priestess of Isis? I could be. Look at me. Could I not be her for you? And could you not also heal me?

LAWRENCE: What pain are you in?

CARESSE: I am lonely, Lawrence. I am in love and lonely. Do you know how that feels? Love me now. They can't see, and even if they did, it wouldn't matter. What would they care? What should they? Please, Lawrence. Touch me. (*Pause*) Well, let me touch you. You don't need to do anything, just trust, trust in the priestess.

She kneels, and reaches out to him.

LAWRENCE: Do not touch me. Oh, God, this endless yearning of women to be the redeemers and resurrectors of their men. It's mere fantasy.

CARESSE: But is this not what your story says?

LAWRENCE: (*Suddenly furious*) It's not an autobiography.

CARESSE: But dare you not live what you preach? You'll just let another man stand firm in your place? Right now, even now, as we speak, they are probably –

LAWRENCE: You hope to turn my anger into lust?

CARESSE: It is your pride I hoped to reach.

LAWRENCE: My pride? Ah. And I thought it was my shame. (*Suddenly exhausted*) Caresse. Thank you. You are very beautiful. It's not you. It is simply now no more for me. And you are right. I only imagine. In truth I have not done the half of what I imagined. Your husband is the opposite. He's hardly imagined half of what he's done. The half in the bright sun he knows, but in the shadows is a man unknown to him.

CARESSE: And what form does that man take?

LAWRENCE: I am not Tiresias, but I will tell you this. Women should not kneel naked over dead men for too long. It is not natural.

Silence. LAWRENCE *closes his eyes against the sun.*

FRIEDA: (*Calling from the distance*) Caresse, can you hear us, come on, come on in!

HARRY: (*Calling*) Lawrence!

CARESSE: Forgive me.

LAWRENCE: Oh, Caresse. There's nothing to forgive.

FRIEDA: (*Calling*) Please, Lorenzo, come and join us, please. Risk it!

HARRY: (*Calling*) Come on, Caresse!

LAWRENCE: Go. I'm more than content here by the water's edge.

She dives into the water, with the cries of greetings from the others. The women still call out his name as they swim into the distance. HARRY *watches him, unseen.*

LAWRENCE: (*Softly*) Don't they understand anything? It would be my death. (*Pause*) What do I do now? What do I ever do? (*Takes out his notebook*) (*Reading*) "She said: 'Oh, don't go! Stay with me on half the island. I will build a house for you and me under the pine trees, where we can live together."' Ridiculous, sounds like some silly *billet doux*. (*Frowns: Amending*) "Build a house… where we can live apart from the whole world." No, no, too… just "I will build a house for you and me under the pine trees, where we can live apart." Cut. Cut. To the quick. "Yet she knew that he would go. And even she wanted the sigh of…" No, no, "Even she wanted the coolness of her own air around her, and the release from anxiety."

LAWRENCE *frowns. A pause. He closes the note-book.*

HARRY: Is that it?

LAWRENCE: (*Startled*) What? Is that what?

HARRY: The last line.

LAWRENCE: Perhaps.

HARRY: *Her* release from anxiety? But isn't it his story? I mean, where is he going for his release?

LAWRENCE: He doesn't know.

HARRY: Doesn't he? But do you?

LAWRENCE: (*Reaching to the towels*) Do you need a towel?

HARRY: No, no, the sun will −

LAWRENCE: Yes, of course it will.

HARRY *sits, and pulls on a string to drag another bottle of champagne out.*

HARRY: *Voila! Une autre bouteille.*

LAWRENCE: Should you not save some? Just in case.

HARRY: A never-ending miraculous supply.

LAWRENCE: What are you like with loaves and fishes?

HARRY: (*Smiling*) You'll see at lunch. (*Turning to the hamper*) Would you like a glass?

LAWRENCE: No.

HARRY: You haven't even touched the picnic. The madeleines are so gentle, full of memories of Proust, and, oh, these apples. They are so tender. Who knows how they find them this time of year. You have to search, always, always search. (*Crunches into one himself*) (*In ecstacy*) Oh, God, yes paradise, I can hear the snake hissing how good it is, is that old villain, so decried, your splendid plumed serpent, Quetzalcoatl? Crossing the world, looking for the sun. Listen, that's it, what I want to... (*Drinks straight from the bottle*) what I saw, Lawrence, in the pool here, well, illumination, it was wondrous, I rose from the dark, and was standing still for a moment in the water, up to the level of my chest, and as the ripples died away, and the whole world flattened out again do you know what I could see on the surface?

LAWRENCE: (*Simply*) The sun.

HARRY: Yes, God, how did you know?

LAWRENCE: Just a guess.

HARRY: The sun. The sun can be seen in the water, the sun does truly disappear into the sea. Into the dark. But of course it's not gone away, it's there submerged, there all the time in the lower depths. Even when the clouds appear and obscure. Still there. And that's when I realised.

LAWRENCE: What?

HARRY: Where his true resurrection lies. Where your man, the man who died, is sailing to.

LAWRENCE: Who says he's sailing anywhere in particular?

HARRY: But he is, isn't he? He may not name it, but he knows his destination. Only a man who has died already can truly know it. Tell me, please. He sets out to sea?

LAWRENCE: (*Quietly*) It's true, there is a boat there, a small boat hidden in the hollow of another cave.

HARRY: And he will take it and row away.

LAWRENCE: (*Quietly but meant*) Do not foresee my end.

HARRY: No, listen to me, Lawrence, please, look I know, I am all too painfully aware what you think of me, that I'm some fool spoilt by gold and it would do me the world of good if my alchemical experiments reversed everything back to copper and clay, and I was sent underground to work with the true thorough-breeds bringing black coal into light of day. And perhaps you are right, I can't deny, but it doesn't change that I have seen… I know where he is heading, him. And you. And me too. Because we are all heading to the same place.

LAWRENCE: Where? Carthage? Byzantium? Whitby Bay?

HARRY: *O mort, vieux capitaine, il est temps! Levons l'ancre!* "O death, old captain, it's time! Raise the anchor!" (*Pause*) Forgive me for quoting Baudelaire. I know you are somewhat sensitive about living artists, but he's been long dead.

LAWRENCE: Yes.

HARRY: And yet he still speaks so directly to our hearts.

LAWRENCE: Yes.

HARRY: And where are we going? What does he say?

LAWRENCE: *Enfer ou Ciel, qu'importe? / Au fond de l'inconnu pour trouver du nouveau.*

HARRY: "Heaven or Hell, who gives a fuck? / To the depths of the unknown to find the new." Fantastic. Death. A fantastic voyage. How can we resist?

LAWRENCE: Some of us are not quite so keen as you to raise the anchor.

HARRY: But it's true, isn't it?

Silence.

LAWRENCE: (*Eventually*) Yes. Thank you. (*Pause*) I think I'll have an apple now.

The women can be heard giggling and splashing.

HARRY: Look at the women, so beautiful. (*Pause*) Should they come with us too?

LAWRENCE: Leave them for a time, Harry. For a time.

HARRY: I can't do that. I don't want to travel alone. (*Rises: Laughing*) I'm coming!

He dives back into the water. Silence. LAWRENCE bites into the apple.

LAWRENCE: *Das ist gut!*

Act Two

As the sounds of the pool fade away.

LAWRENCE: Come on, Lawrence. Pen. Paper. Always to hand. Why? (*Pause*) I don't care.

He opens his notebook and begins to write. At first he simply murmurs to himself and then nods. He takes his time.

LAWRENCE: 'The man pulled slowly out, to get into the current which set down the coast, and would carry him in silence. The man who had died rowed slowly on with the current and" spoke? Whispered? No. The man "laughed to himself" I hear it so clearly. 'I have sowed the seed of my life and my resurrection, and put my touch for ever upon the choice woman of this day, and I carry her perfume in my flesh like the essence of roses. She is dear to me in the middle of my being. But the gold and flowing serpent is coiling up again, to sleep at the root of my tree. So let the boat carry me. Tomorrow is another day". Yes. (*Pause: gently in imitation of* HARRY) Heaven or hell, who gives a fuck? Oh. (*Softly*) Frieda. (*Sighs, bites into the apple, and begins to cough.*)

FRIEDA: (*Voice panicking*) Lorenzo! Lorenzo!

LAWRENCE: It's all right, my love.

He puts his handkerchief to his mouth. It is now blood-stained.

LAWRENCE: Only laughing. (*He's totally exhausted*) I'm coming in. I'm coming in.

He stands uncertain. As the lights change and the intro. to Bessie Smith's Empty Bed Blues, FRIEDA *appears, now in black, widows weeds. She holds a champagne glass. She smiles gently at* LAWRENCE.

BESSIE SMITH: I woke up this morning

With an awful aching head (repeat)
My new man had left me
Just a room and an empty bed

FRIEDA: Lorenzo died just before the following Easter, at Vence, in the south of France. He was forty-four. I was of course by his bedside. His last words were —

LAWRENCE: *(Softly)* Hold me, hold me. I don't know where I am.

She approaches LAWRENCE *and gently puts her arm around him leading him to sit by the picnic cloth.*

BESSIE SMITH: Bought me a coffee grinder
Got the best one I could find (repeat)
Thought he could grind my coffee
'Cos he had a brand new grind

As they move over, CARESSE *appears, also in widow's black and sits by the pool with a white towelling robe emblazoned* Hotel des Artistes. *She hums along with Bessie, and holds up the robe as* HARRY *rises up from the pool behind it.*

BESSIE SMITH: He's a deep sea diver
With a stroke that can't go wrong
He can touch the bottom
And his wind holds out so long.

CARESSE: Lawrence was right about Harry.

A shot rings out and reverberates through the trees.

CARESSE: Nine months later, on December 9th, 1929, in the *Hotel des Artistes* in New York, Harry shot his new paramour, Josephine Bigelow — the woman he called his Fire Princess — and then turned the gun against his own head. He really didn't want to go alone.

Holding hands she takes him to join the others, as FRIEDA *begins handing out madeleines and fruit.*

FRIEDA: Lorenzo called his death —

LAWRENCE: "The last sort of cocktail excitement."

But he smiles up at HARRY *as he joins them.*

BESSIE SMITH: He knows how to thrill me
And he thrills me night and day —
He's got a new way of loving
Almost takes my breath away.

LAWRENCE: *(Without any trace of anger)* Frieda married her lover, our former gardener, Angelo Ravagli, and with the money from the D. H. Lawrence estate bought him out of his commission in Mussolini's army.

HARRY: Caresse married an actor, Selbert Young, young by name, young by nature, sixteen years her junior. He was a cowboy in B-movies.

He grins and hands her a glass of champagne. HARRY *gently joins in with* BESSIE.

BESSIE SMITH: He's got that sweet something
I told my girlfriend Lou
For the way she's drinking
She must have gone and tried him too …

As the sun descends and the pool behind now seems to have become a rising sea and the song ends —

CARESSE: Harry and I did publish an edition of his Easter

Tale – *The Escaped Cock.*

FRIEDA: Lawrence wept when he saw it. He said it was so, so beautiful.

As they picnic, slowly the stage begins to glow. The scene suffused with the flush of rose. Blackout.

The End

The Fox… and the Little Vixen

Introduction

Coming from a working-class family in Nottingham, with dreams of being a writer, it's inevitable that from my earliest teens I fell under the sway of D. H. Lawrence. *Sons and Lovers* seemed written solely for me, a remarkably prescient insight into my own life and aspirations. At university I directed his wonderful play *The Daughter-in-Law* before starting an M.A. on the man. It became a key influence on *Touched*, my play about the women of Nottingham in wartime. And over the years, apart from being a major influence in form and content, he's made various "guest appearances" in a number of my plays. *Divine Gossip* (RSC) followed him through his final years, and *Moving Pictures* my autobiographical play about kids trying to make a Laurentian "sex" film in the 60s (Royal Court Theatre) was haunted by him. Indeed, recently he literally turns up as a spirit in my comedy for the Nottingham Playhouse on the "return of Brian Clough" – *The Spirit of the Man. Empty Bed Blues* is set in the last year of Lawrence's life. But I've never attempted an adaptation of his work, and even now, I'm afraid I still haven't. Nor indeed was it ever my intention. Lawrence seems to me too challenging, too argumentative a writer for another writer simply, meekly, to find a way to put his work into another form. That's not to say there are not highly successful adaptations only that for me what I find most exciting about him is that I can't sit still and stay silent. Lawrence demands a response. He refuses to leave you alone. The choice is straight-forward with him – either you are forced into a passive submission (and we know how little respect he felt for those who "gave in") or he prods and pushes at you until you are finally forced to "break through" – to search for your own vision, and, most significantly, to discover your own true voice. And that, for good or ill, is what I have done here. My vision, whilst influenced, as any child is by that of his father, any artist is by that of his mentor, is different from Lawrence's. And my way to open up the piece was to add a second voice – this time a musical one – to the debate. In the same year that Lawrence published *The Fox*, The great Czech composer, Janacek, composed his opera on the fox *The Cunning Little Vixen* inspired by an almost diametrically opposed vision of life.

Introduction

This play *The Fox… and the Little Vixen* is born out of my own meeting and imaginative journey with these two men of extraordinary talent. It has been a genuine privilege and a pleasure and I thank Tangere Arts for generously supporting me through this time. The piece, like those artists' works, is highly subjective and hopefully will stimulate a response in you. I hope you enjoy it, and that those fellow Lawrence lovers amongst you will not see it as anything but what it is – an imaginative response created out of total respect to a great artist.

Stephen Lowe

Characters

Ellie March
Jill Bamford
Henry Grenfel

The time – now.

The place – outside a small farmhouse in Derbyshire.

The first performance of *The Fox… and the Little Vixen* was given at the Derby Playhouse on 30 September 2005 by Tangere Arts in association with Derby Playhouse, Arts Council England and The Esmee Fairburn Foundation.

The cast was as follows:

Jill Bamford – Ava Hunt
Ellie March – Tanya Myers
Henry Grenfel – Jarrod Cooke

Director – Maggie Ford
Designer – Tricia Donnison
Costumes and Props – Julieann Heskin
Company Manager – Paul Foxcroft
Music – Lewis Gibson

Act One

Scene One

Outside the farm house.

Dark.

Music: Janacek, opening prelude.

Fade lights up on –

Derbyshire. The garden of a stone cottage, with the backdoor to the house upstage.

JILL who sits by the side of a small table, gazing out, CD remote in hand, listening to the music. Whilst a sunny day it's still sharp, and she has a thin shawl over her knees and a paperback poetry book in her lap. Her eyes flick from side to side as though she's seeing the various insects, animals, indicated by the music. She hums along with the music. She is happy.

She fades out the music only to find it "mirrored" in reality by the sounds of the country- the bird song, clucking hens, distant bleat of lambs. It makes her even happier. She grins and picks up the poetry book and mumbles the words to herself.

Behind her, ELLIE arrives.

ELLIE (a Londoner) appears with a few eggs in a wicker basket. She's in T-shirt and jeans and leather jacket. JILL is all together neater. Both women are in their late thirties. They have clearly decided to ignore the class difference between them. JILL shifts in a moment from high, febrile energy and excitement to sudden exhaustion. Almost mid-sentence she can lose her energy. ELLIE, whilst more pragmatic and solidly paced, can herself fall into dark reveries of a distant kind. In short, ELLIE is a deep alto to JILL's soprano diva. ELLIE is almost endlessly busy, but shows not the least sign of resentment for that.

ELLIE: (*Softly*) Jill.

JILL: (*Not turning to her*) Listen:
  If she would come to me here
  Now the sunken swaths
  Are glittering paths
  To the sun, and the swallows cut clear
  Into the setting sun! If she came to me here!

ELLIE: Jill.

JILL: *If she would come to me now,*
  Before the last-mown harebells are dead
  While that vetch clump still burns red!
  Before all the bats have dropped from the bough
  To cool in the night: if she came to me now!
  (*Glancing at her for the first time*) What do you think?

ELLIE: (*Smiling*) What's a vetch clump when it's at 'home?

JILL: (*Hesitates*) It's poetry, Ellie. Poetry.

ELLIE: (*Lightly*) Oh, well, that answers everything.

  A momentary cloud and JILL *gives an involuntary shiver.* ELLIE
  quickly slides her own jacket around JILL's *shoulders.*

JILL: It's by D. H. Lawrence. It's called "Dog Tired". Rather apt
  for me, don't you think?

ELLIE: You'll be all right.

JILL: Yes.

  The sun re-appears. The bleat of lambs.

JILL: The newborn. (*Smiles*) Listen to them. So ecstatic just to
  be alive. Have you ever felt like that?

ELLIE: Maybe. In my biker days.

JILL: (*Carefully*) Was that with someone in particular? (*a beat*) Who was he?

ELLIE: Called Norton.

JILL: Was he… (*Grins*)… good?

ELLIE: Ye', great, once I'd stripped him down, and done an oil change. Norton's a motorbike, love. Listen, Jill, we've got a problem and a 'alf here. I was planning to do us an omelette before you go to your lot's rehearsal but we're down to two eggs here. God knows where the hens are hiding them. I swear they're doing their own deals with the supermarket. We've got to get proper fences up.

JILL: We've only been here a couple of months. It takes time.

ELLIE: And money. If we're going to turn this into your dream, we're playing it tight.

JILL: When the barn's done, the workshops and guests will pay for the upkeep.

ELLIE: And will these guests fork out in advance so we can get the conversion done, cos we're a long way off levitating above the azaleas.

JILL: I've still a bit left over from my flat. And I'll get some design work round here.

ELLIE: One thing I have learned is that nobody round 'ere is going to pay for an architect. All they're after is some cowboy to botch up a cheap conversion so they can flog it on as a second home. Even they are hard enough to find. I could do with Jessie James and his gang meself to get that new floor down in the barn.

JILL: I'm not much use, am I?

ELLIE: I'm not moaning. If I hadn't met you, the bloody mess I was in, I would have signed up with the Foreign Legion if they'd guaranteed me Tampax. This is a lot better than that, believe me. Only…

JILL: What?

ELLIE: S'all right. My problem. I'll run you down early then you can catch a bite before the rehearsal.

JILL: It's only a tech meeting, sort out the set. (*Laughs*) Still can't believe they bought the idea. Country opera society all with Save the Hunt stickers all over their four by fours and they agreed to do Janacek's *The Cunning Little Vixen*. You'd think they would have seen the paradox, wouldn't you?

ELLIE: Most of them are townies anyway.

JILL: Yes, but…

ELLIE: You ready?

JILL *clicks the controls of a small mini-system. The opening of the opera.*

ELLIE: Oh, bloody 'ell – I can't stand operas. They always take too long to die.

JILL: Have you ever seen one?

ELLIE: Give me *Grease* any day.

JILL: (*Smiling*) I had realised that. No, come on listen please. Try to see it. Janacek opens like Lawrence with a hunter who's so dog tired he lies down to sleep in the forest, and around him, listen you can hear them-

ELLIE: Where?

JILL: And the lovely little vixen cub there, she sees a frog for the first time and then she's hypnotised by the flight of the Blue Dragonfly; she's never seen anything so beautiful. And the frog jumps away onto the chest of the hunter, who wakes up and sees the vixen. But does he shoot, no, he grabs her and says – (*spoken*) "My kids will like you, you'll help to keep them quiet". Keep them quiet? Dream on. She's going to give them hell!

ELLIE: That I can believe. (*Switches music off*) We lost another two hens last night, Jill.

JILL: (*A beat*) I don't want to talk about it. You know how I feel.

ELLIE: We're trying to make money out of them. Old Foxy uses us like a drive-in McDonalds. If we are to survive, he's got to go.

JILL: He's as much right to live as us.

ELLIE: Oh ye', and what about equal rights for hens?

JILL: Look, I know we're in the country now, and I'm not trying to impose city values on it. But just because it's the country doesn't mean we can't be civilised, does it?

ELLIE: And you figure the fox is going to go for that and say thank you, can I just order one for Sunday lunch and for the rest of the week I'll settle for salad? All he cares about is going on killing.

JILL: Surviving.

ELLIE: He's got the same problem as us then.

JILL: That's my point.

ELLIE: (*Eventually*) You haven't seen him. I have.

JILL: (*Startled*) What?

ELLIE: The other night. Down on the edge of forest over there. It was dusk. I figured he'd be coming over for his take-away. I saw a movement through the trees, a blur of bronze, and suddenly it stilled. I practically walked up to him, if I'd had a gun, but I don't know, even then he might not have run away.

JILL: What do you mean?

ELLIE: (*Quietly*) He just sat up and looked at me. Dead composed. His tail flicked round him, like he was modelling for one of them porcelain ornaments your gran might think lovely. Just looked at me. Animals don't really ever look at you. Look up for food, or to check where your hand is for a stroke but ... he just looked at me, calm as a cucumber, one of them looks that are ... (*Trying to laugh*) I don't know, what I'd call... leery... dead leery... stripping you down, leaving you burning naked and... (*Pause*) I wanted to kill that bugger but... He was so beautiful, Jill...

JILL: What happened?

ELLIE: After he'd looked enough, after he'd stripped me, after I was of no more interest, he just turned tail and sauntered off.

JILL: (*Grinning*) Just like a man.

JILL *stands and puts on a crash helmet.*

ELLIE: (*To herself*) Yes, but next time, Mr Fox. Next time.

Light change. Mist. Drizzle. Early morning. The overture continues under –

Scene Two

A clearing in the forest.

Just before dawn. ELLIE is huddled under a blanket. The music stops. A fox is calling that strange primal sound. She makes a similar guttural cry as she sleeps. Then slowly she stirs from her dream.

ELLIE: No, no, get out, get out of here. I warn you, just get out, and how dare you… (*Shakes her head*) I won't have you… I won't be looked at… what do you think I am, do you think I like…

As she rallies. The sharp snap of a twig underfoot echoes through the still forest. The music suddenly stops. She's on the alert. From under the blanket she produces an old shotgun. She's hardly clear on how it works.

ELLIE: Bugger. Bugger!

She finally clicks the gun into ready and aims.

ELLIE: Right, you bugger! Die!

The fox cry suddenly mingles with a more human one.

HENRY: (*Voice*) No! No! Don't shoot!

ELLIE: What?

HENRY: (*Voice*) Please. Please don't shoot.

HENRY, *a half-naked slim young man in his early twenties rises up from the ground gripping his sleeping bag around him.*

HENRY: (*Terrified*) I surrender. I'm a bit short right now on a white flag, but…

ELLIE: Wha'…

She stares at him in total disbelief.

HENRY: (*Shaking*) Just put gun down love, please. I can't take no more folk taking pot shots at me, eh? Just put the gun down please....

ELLIE: (*Trembling*) I thought you were... what the fuck are you.... I mean I, God, I could have killed you.

HENRY: (*Realising he's safe*) S'all right. It's okay, love. It 'appens all the time. Lots of folks get shot in accidents like this. Bloke sees a bush move, and blast, that's you away. You have to be double careful 'fore you shoot. (*trying to make light*) Or you end up peppering some poor lover's bum and making him limp 'ome.

He laughs, then as the light improves, he remains still, looking at her. Silence.

ELLIE: (*Sharply*) Stop. Stop staring at me!

HENRY: It's you... you looking at me... I mean... (*pause*) Sorry.

But the look is only broken by the sudden arrival of JILL in dressing gown and carpet slippers. At first she doesn't see the young man.

JILL: (*Terrified*) What's going on? What have you done? Have you killed him? (*Gaining no response*) Where did you get the gun?

HENRY: (*Moving on*) From the barn, innit? Hidden under the floor. Next to the sink.

JILL *turns in amazement to take in* HENRY. *He quietly takes the gun from* ELLIE *and unloads it.*

HENRY: He allers hid it there. Thought the kids din't know.

Din't they hell as like.

JILL: What… who…

ELLIE *shakes her head.*

HENRY: Morning.

JILL: Morn… what, what, what are you doing here?

HENRY: I coun't find a bed for the night, tried the Black Swan but wi' all these trippers and walkers… anyroad I'm used to roughing it in the open so…

JILL: But why here?

HENRY: I come to have a look.

ELLIE: At what? At us? What have you heard, there are freaks living up on the hill?

HENRY: No, no. Nowt like, no. Me granddad lived here. Grenfel. Albert Grenfel.

JILL: (*Pause*) I brought the place in auction after he died.

HENRY: Ye' I heard. We coun't have kept it in family anyroad. He owed all the money to the bank. Place had long since made no profit. Does it now?

JILL: It will.

HENRY: Brill. Only I used to come here as a kid. Being army family, never stayed in one place long enough to know the way home. So this sort of… when I thought about it… this was me home. Whatever that means, eh? So I just fancied seeing it again.

Act One

JILL: Why didn't you come to the house?

HENRY: Din't want to go disturbing you.

ELLIE: Disturbing us? You bloody frightened me to death!

HENRY: Likewise. Well, almost. (*Smiles*)

JILL: Well, you'd better come up to the house now. Having tried to kill you, the least we can do is offer you breakfast. Ellie, better see if you can find some eggs.

ELLIE pauses for a moment, speechless, and then strides off furious.

JILL: Bit of a shock for her.

She smiles at the young man. He nods and smiles back. She follows after ELLIE. HENRY stands silhouetted in the rising dawn. As the fox cries out. He raises the gun to his shoulder and mimes a shot. He laughs. Music.

Scene Three

Outside the farmhouse.

ELLIE is laying out the breakfast with no degree of delicacy. As JILL comes out with an old tea-service.

JILL: What's got into you?

ELLIE: It's a bloody daft idea.

JILL: What is?

ELLIE: Inviting naked men for breakfast.

JILL: You normally boot them out the night before do you? That was a joke.

ELLIE: Not with my life it isn't.

JILL: Come on. Just five minutes of country courtesy.

ELLIE: We don't know anything about him.

JILL: We know he's called Grenfel.

As HENRY *appears in t-shirt, jeans, and combat jacket, carrying the shotgun.* ELLIE *immediately takes it from him, and determinately "breaks it".*

HENRY: Henry Grenfel.

JILL: Jill Banford. And this is Ellie March.

HENRY: March?

JILL: March comes in like a lion and goes out like a lamb.

ELLIE: Don't you believe it.

She holds out her hands for the cartridges. He gives them back.

JILL: Sit down, please.

HENRY: Listen, I don't mean to barge in. I were fit in the woods. As a kid, I used to camp out there at nights.

ELLIE: How long are you planning to take up residence this time?

HENRY: Just the night. Then I were off.

JILL: To where?

HENRY: Dunno. Walking holiday. This were the main point. From here, nowhere in particular.

JILL: That's where Ellie dreams of going isn't it?

ELLIE: What?

JILL: You dream of getting on your motorbike one day and setting off into the wide blue yonder.

ELLIE: I've never said that. Never.

A momentary tension between the two women. Henry tries to cover –

HENRY: So… You've got a motorbike then?

ELLIE: Yes.

HENRY: What kind?

ELLIE: Just a Suzuki 1200.

HENRY: (*Impressed*) Just?

Silence. As JILL *offers him tea.*

JILL: Sugar's on the tray.

HENRY: Ta. These cups were my grandma's.

JILL: We found them all wrapped up in paper at the bottom of the dresser.

HENRY: Aye. You would. They were her Sunday best.

ELLIE: Did they keep hens?

HENRY: That's how they scratched a living.

ELLIE: And what did your granddad do about Mr Fox then?

JILL: Leave it, Ellie.

HENRY: He went wi'out sleep is the answer to that. He'd be up most nights. And he'd take us kids wi' 'im, teach us how to shoot proper.

JILL: At least the gun was in the hands of someone who knew what he was doing.

HENRY: It dun't stop accidents happening. Same as in war. In the heat of the moment, you're just as likely to get shot up by your own side.

ELLIE: You in the army?

HENRY: Aye. So… I see you're doing up the barn.

JILL: Trying to. But the local builders have let us down. We need to get the joists in before we can really get moving. I've got big plans for it, I'm an architect, and I want it to become a real fusion of modern, ecological, design and traditional craftsmanship.

HENRY: So you've got the vision, like. (*To* ELLIE) And you?

ELLIE: I'm all right doing things.

HENRY: Does it matter what?

ELLIE: (*Eventually*) Not really.

JILL: Ellie's running herself down. She's really our master builder.

HENRY: Right.

ELLIE: I'm just a pair of hired hands.

HENRY: And could you do with another pair to get them joists up?

ELLIE: What?

HENRY: I'm willing to gi' it a go.

ELLIE: No, no, no, we couldn't –

JILL: Hang on, Ellie, you said you couldn't manage it on your own, and we'll be held up for months waiting for the locals.

ELLIE: He's not looking for a job. The lad's on holiday, or leave, or something.

HENRY: Better exercise than walking.

JILL: So you think you might be interested?

ELLIE: I don't need any help, thanks.

HENRY: Sorry, I'm barging in again.

JILL: Not at all.

ELLIE: It's not a five minute job. There's all the crossbeams to fit, the damp proofing, the joists to be laid, then the flooring to –

JILL: A couple of days maybe.

ELLIE: And we haven't a room for guests. Not yet.

JILL: He could crash out in the spare room for a few nights.

ELLIE: You couldn't swing a cat in there.

HENRY: I'll be all right outside.

JILL: Can't have you catching pneumonia.

ELLIE: And half the time we haven't even got hot water.

HENRY: (*Smiles*) Be like the old days.

JILL: There you go. And of course we'll pay you.

ELLIE: Wha'!

HENRY: Oh, no, no, don't be daft. Bed and board. Be a treat just to be back here for five minutes. (*To* ELLIE) But you sure? I don't want to get under your feet.

ELLIE: (*Grimly*) No. It's fine.

HENRY: Great. Well, I'll go get my gear.

He goes.

ELLIE: Have you gone barking mad or what?

JILL: What?

ELLIE: You practically invited him to move in.

JILL: Is that a bigger mistake than you trying to shoot him?

ELLIE: Could be.

JILL: Now you're being really silly, Ellie. Come on, we need help. And lo and behold, what turns up – (*Grinning*) the answer to a maiden's prayer.

ELLIE: Is that what he is?

JILL: Lighten up. He's a boy, he's hardly out of short pants.

ELLIE: He knows how to use a gun.

JILL: Well, that might be useful.

ELLIE: You've changed your tune. Come on, Jill, think eh? What's in this for him? What's this little lad of yours after? Just a bit of scrumping, jar full of newts, a bag of crisps, and a few laughs?

JILL: Well, frankly, Ellie, a few laughs wouldn't harm any of us.

ELLIE stares at her. Silence.

JILL: (*Suddenly exhausted*) I think I need a rest. Wake me in an hour?

ELLIE: You're the boss.

JILL: Oh come on, Ellie, it's a beautiful day. Risk a smile.

HENRY returns with his rucksack.

JILL: I'm just going for a little nap. The sergeant major here will show you to your quarters.

JILL goes. Silence. ELLIE starts to tidy up. HENRY starts to help.

ELLIE: I can manage.

He backs off.

HENRY: So… er… are you two sisters then?

ELLIE: Do we look like sisters?

The answer is clearly no. Silence.

HENRY: So how did you two… pal up like then eh?

ELLIE: She advertised.

HENRY: Kind of Lonely Hearts type of thing?

ELLIE: What's that mean?

HENRY: Nothing, I was just –

ELLIE: If it was Lonely Hearts I wouldn't hide it. I don't give a sod what people think.

HENRY: Fair enough.

ELLIE: (*Pause*) (*Reluctantly*) She's not well, got M.E. Couldn't take the pace of London any more. This was a dream she had. And she needed somebody with a pair of hands.

HENRY: And you?

ELLIE: I had me own reasons for leaving town.

HENRY: Right. Got you. See the same thing in the army. The oddest blokes pal up together. But they're there for each other, constant back up. Covering all the time. (*Pause*) But folk die. Back up or no.

He looks at her. Silence.

HENRY: I'll just dump these inside. Then I'm ready for action, sarge.

He goes inside. She turns to watch him go. The sound of the fox calling. She seems not to hear it at first. As the lights change to night. She shivers, turns towards it source, looks back towards the cottage. Then she makes a decision, as the lights change to night. She picks up the shotgun, and snaps it ready. She's getting more proficient.

Scene Four

Outside the farmhouse.

Loud music: *Janacek, the entrance of the fox.*

In the darkness the glittering face of a fox glimmers lighted from below by oil-lamps from behind the table. ELLIE stands rooted to the spot. She seems caught in its stare. The head of a similar magical vixen appears, also watching her, then turns to stare up at the fox, finally resting her head against his shoulder. ELLIE is sweating, almost faint. Silence. The vixen makes the softest of calls. The fox breaks the stare and turns to his partner.

ELLIE: *(Furious)* What the fuck are you two playing at?

Laughing, HENRY in the fox mask rises up, swigging back a bottle of beer, JILL by his side in the little vixen mask. Both are well drunk and giggling. She's finishing off the second half of a bottle of wine. ELLIE slams the shotgun onto the table, and switches off the C.D. player. Silence.

JILL: *(Looking up)* What's the matter?

ELLIE: What do you mean what's the matter?

JILL: I asked you first.

ELLIE: What's going on here?

JILL: We're just trying out my masks for Mr and Mrs Fox. Before I take them in for the costume check.

ELLIE: *(Confused)* I didn't know she had a husband.

JILL: That's because you won't listen to the opera.

ELLIE: Ye', well I do have better things to do.

JILL: Like kill the fox?

ELLIE: Ye' right, whilst you are pratting in daft masks, that bugger's eating all our profit.

JILL: You know how I feel.

HENRY: But she's right.

ELLIE: I don't need you for back up.

But JILL *is paying more attention to him than her.*

HENRY: I'll get him for you.

JILL: (*Eventually*) If you must.

ELLIE: It's not down to him. I'm the one here trying to make us a living.

JILL: And I'm the one trying to make us a life.

She looks up smiling at ELLIE. *Sudden sound of chaos, chickens screaming.* ELLIE *seizes the shotgun and is gone.*

JILL: I hate it. This is… (*Takes off her mask – in panic*) This is what I hate.

HENRY *rises. He tries to put his arm around the woman, she shrugs him off. He stands not knowing what to do. With her hands over her ears, she finally manages to break away, towards the house.* HENRY *doesn't know which way to turn.*

As ELLIE *quietly returns, with broken gun. She picks off a few feathers and watches them float through the air. She turns to* HENRY.

ELLIE: Take that silliness off.

HENRY *takes off the mask.*

HENRY: Much lost? (*Gaining no answer*) She's very upset your...
(*Pause*) Did you get a shot off?

ELLIE: You know I didn't.

HENRY: Did you see him?

Silence. She sits and pours herself a glass of wine. She studies the vixen mask.

ELLIE: (*Quietly*) She's mad you know. (*Pause*) (*Softly*) If she had her way, she'd turn Mr Fox into a pet. Let him get his feet under the table and play hopscotch with the hens. And then she'd educate him, and teach him how to sing.

HENRY: He sings already. But 'appens it's not a tune she fancies. (*Pause*) You don't never tame foxy. You can lay his favourite food out wi' knife, fork and napkin, and he'll say grace and eat all you gi' him, smack his lips, and go straight off to party amongst the hens. He's a natural killer. It's not a hobby. You can't convert him to flower arranging. Bloody shame, cos he's a beautiful bugger but that's the choice. Kill or gi' in to him. He knows that. It's just us what has to learn. (*Pause*) Had you not better tend to her Ladyship?

ELLIE: Her what?

HENRY: I meant nought by it. Just one of them things you say.

A distant cry.

ELLIE: There he is again.

HENRY: That in't him. That's her. The missis. Desperate. Calling. That's the song you need to learn if you want the fox to come running.

Silence. He smiles.

ELLIE: And what's she wanting?

HENRY: Not for me to say. That's a woman thing. (*Breaking the spell*) I'd best turn in.

He goes inside. ELLIE remains. Light change. A distant growl building into the sound of a motorbike approaching at high speed, then quickly changing down and stopping.

Scene Five

Outside the farm.

A glorious mid-summer day. JILL enters for a moment hardly recognisable in crash helmet and leather jacket and carrying shopping. ELLIE turns to face her. HENRY also in full crash helmet appears by her side with more shopping. A beat. JILL does a crazy jig.

JILL: (*Muffled*) First night presents. (*Lifts the visor*) First night presents! Lots of frogs!

ELLIE *does not respond.*

ELLIE: (*To* HENRY) You took my bike.

JILL: Our bike, Ellie. (*Taking out a selection of croaking frogs*) Look at what I found for our leading –

ELLIE: I needed the bike.

JILL: What for?

ELLIE: Never mind what for. I had things to do on that bike. It's not for going on jaunts. It's –

JILL: I know, it's a workhorse. It ploughs the field and scatters.

ELLIE: I'm not saying it's a combine fucking harvester, just I needed it. You could at least have asked.

HENRY: I'm sorry.

JILL: Not his fault. I just had to check how the set building was getting on, and you weren't around –

ELLIE: I wasn't very far away.

JILL: And anyway Henry has offered to help with the lighting –

ELLIE: Is there anything you can't turn your hand to?

HENRY: I try.

JILL: And we need all the help we can.

ELLIE: So do I. I can't put in a floor on my own.

HENRY: Well, I'm here now.

ELLIE: How come you're got all this free time? Don't you have your walk to finish? Or get back to your base?

JILL: Ellie, come on, we open tomorrow and then it's all done and dusted by the end of the week. And he's really useful. He can talk to the old blokes here, they understand him.

HENRY: They remember me.

JILL: And more importantly they listen to him. He got things sorted in no time.

ELLIE: Ye', so why did it take you all day then?

HENRY: It didn't.

JILL: But it's such a beautiful day. And everyone needs to escape once in a while.

ELLIE: Do they?

JILL: So when Henry suggested a bag of chips and-

HENRY: (*Grinning*) Mushy peas-

JILL: And I thought I really do need a leather jacket of my own.

ELLIE: (*To* HENRY) You went into Matlock?

HENRY: Yes.

ELLIE: (*To* JILL) And the bike shop?

JILL: Something wrong with that?

ELLIE: That's *my* bike shop.

JILL: That's silly, Ellie, you're being really silly.

ELLIE: He's not insured.

JILL: We can sort that out.

ELLIE: What's the point? He'll be gone in a few days.

HENRY: I'll take these inside.

He goes.

JILL: What's going on, Nell?

ELLIE: You're asking me?

JILL: We just went for a ride.

ELLIE: Did he do a ton? Did he get you going? Bounce you back into life?

JILL: As a matter of fact, he was really sweet. He went dead slow.

ELLIE: Sensitive. That's nice.

JILL: What you suggesting?

ELLIE: Has he picked his wallpaper out yet?

JILL: Oh come on, he'll be going back to the army soon. As soon as he has recuperated.

ELLIE: And who said he was ill? Did he?

JILL: Unless we can talk him out of it.

ELLIE: (*Floored*) What? Sorry, am I missing something here, talk him out of what?

JILL: Going back to the army.

ELLIE: Wha'? Is that…. Is this some kind of crusade? Come on, you don't expect me to buy that ballocks, do you? That's not the game you're playing here.

JILL: So what am I playing?

ELLIE: You're flirting with the boy.

JILL: Flirting?

ELLIE: God, It's too embarrassing to watch. I keep wanting to throw a bucket of water over you. I mean, do you seriously reckon he's going to fancy you? You're old enough to be his mother.

JILL: Thank you.

ELLIE: What's going on in your head… you've got too much time on your hands, you don't imagine a lad like him gives a fuck about opera, he's just doing it to get inside your knickers-

JILL: Oh, so he does fancy me then after all, does he? As long as I keep my teeth in?

ELLIE: It's more like he might fancy his family estate back.

JILL: Now he's a gold digger? I can't keep pace. Come on, Ellie, tell me what's going on in *your* head?

ELLIE: I'll tell you what this is, I'll tell you exactly what we have here. We have a woman making a right pratt of herself. And I don't want to watch it.

JILL: (*Eventually*) You're jealous.

ELLIE: Oh, ye', and who am I supposed to be jealous of?

JILL: (*Pauses*) That's a very interesting question.

As HENRY *returns. He catches the two women in a stare-out.* ELLIE *breaks first and goes off towards the field.* JILL *turns smiling.*

JILL: Thank you for a lovely day.

HENRY: Listen, I don't want to muck things up between you two.

JILL: You're not. Quite the contrary. (*Smiles*) I'm tired. But in the nicest possible way. I think I need to rest.

She's unsteady. He reaches out to her. She gently pushes him away.

HENRY: You sure you don't need me?

JILL: Absolutely positive. (*Starts to move inside*) Don't worry about Ellie. Her bark is worse than her bite. (*Smiles*) And her singing's worse than both.

HENRY: I haven't heard her sing.

JILL: Count yourself lucky.

She goes. HENRY *watches her leave, and then looks in the direction* ELLIE *went. Fade up the (distant choir) prelude to the arrival of Mr Fox.*

Scene Six

The clearing in the forest.

Dappled by the sunlight, ELLIE *is chopping wood, in her T-shirt. She sluices water over her head. She comes to, knowing* HENRY *has appeared behind her. She turns to his stare.*

ELLIE: Aren't your services needed elsewhere?

HENRY: Where? (*Pause*) Oh, you mean the show thing. They can cope wi'out me for a bit.

ELLIE: Unlike your little ladies, eh?

Silence. She stares at him. He doesn't look away. Eventually –

ELLIE: Didn't have you down for an opera man.

HENRY: Tek it or leave it.

ELLIE: Daft story though in't it? All them singing foxes and hens and things.

HENRY: Think it's quite funny actually. And a bit moving in parts.

ELLIE: Do you now?

HENRY: (*Pause*) You figure I don't have feelings, don't you?

ELLIE: I know a nice story about foxes and hens if you're into that. Learned it at school. Yellow book two. Hen sees the fox coming, jumps up into the tree, reckoning on the fox being no great climber-

HENRY: Which is true.

ELLIE: Foxy makes no effort anyway. Just hangs about for a chat like, nice weather, blah blah but all the time he's chatting he's slowly spinning round chasing his own tail, gradually picking up speed, round and round under the hen on the branch, and the strange thing is-

HENRY: It's the hen gets dizzy not him. And falls into his open mouth. (*Grins*) I remember them kids stories allers had a point, and just in case you missed it they wrote it up big on last page. They should do it with grown-up stories, save us simple sods from having to ponder. So come on, what's the point?

ELLIE: (*Quietly*) The point is, whatever the game is you're playing, I'm not going to let you fuck her over.

HENRY: Don't know what you're going on about.

ELLIE: Oh come on, I'm saying she might act like some daft smitten kid, but we both know she's no spring chicken.

HENRY: (*Laughs*) What is she then? Some old broiler?

ELLIE: If you like.

HENRY: Like yo'?

ELLIE: If you like.

HENRY: That how you see yoursen?

ELLIE: I'm not talking about me.

HENRY: No, but I am. And I'll tell you someat straight, I don't see you like that. You want to know how I see you? Look at me. Look at how I see you. Come on. Look at me.

She turns and stares at him. Eventually –

ELLIE: Don't go playing your games with me.

HENRY: I've wanted you since I first clapped eyes on you. And you knew it.

ELLIE: Don't know what you're talking about.

HENRY: You've been calling me. Calling. Why else do you think I've stayed?

ELLIE: You've got it all upside down. Don't pride yourself

that –

HENRY: Hang on, gi' me my go to make a point. It in't easy this. Right. You've had one go at killing me. Here's a second chance on same spot. One wrong word from you and you've shot me dead. (*Pause*). Here goes. It in't her I want. I want you. I want yo' stripped bare, want yo' yelping like that vixen through the night for me. I'd kill for yo', and kill meself if I can't have yo'. But you want me. I know you do. You've beads of sweat running now between your breasts. I can feel it on my own chest. I can feel the beat of your heart inside me. Tell me I'm wrong. Go on. Tell me.

ELLIE: (*A beat*) You're mad. I don't know what you are after, I don't own this place, what have you got to gain?

HENRY: Don't dare do that to me. Kill me, if it must be, but with respect. Don't set the dogs on me. I've done nowt to warrant that. Answer me question. Am I wrong? Tell me.

She seems locked into his stare. Silence. The cry of the foxes together. She turns away towards them.

HENRY: Leave them. Let them be.

Silence. She turns back to face his stare. She touches her heart. Blackout.

Scene Seven

Outside the farm.

Music: Janacek, the hunter's last attempt to kill the vixen.

Night. ELLIE sits alone, the C.D. player on her knee, and a glass full of wine in her hand. She seems totally absorbed in the music. For once we hear the singers in Czech. The shotgun is nearby. JILL enters in her kimono dressing gown.

JILL: What are you doing out here?

ELLIE: What's going on?

JILL: My question.

ELLIE: No, I mean now, this bit, in the opera.

JILL: What do you care?

ELLIE: (*Insistent*) Tell me.

JILL: (*Listening*) You're near the end. The hunter's laid a trap for the vixen, but she's too clever to fall for it. (*Pause*) And then suddenly a wild shot into the dark kills her. But nobody knows. It's a kind of an accident. And none of the humans are even aware of it. But slowly she's surrounded by the cubs, her children, her own little vixens.

ELLIE: She has children?

JILL: That's the whole point of what becomes the final scene. About renewal. The eternal cycle of life and death.

ELLIE: (*Quietly*) She has children.

JILL: Are you okay?

ELLIE: And where is Mister Fox through all this?

JILL: (*Shakes her head*) We never see him again.

ELLIE: Why do all operas have to end with a dead woman?

JILL: This doesn't, that's the whole point. (*Takes the controls*) Listen. The last scene. It seems like a reprise of the first- the dog tired hunter enters again, but he is much older, nearing the end of his own life, and it's not been all he dreamt but now although he's spent his entire life in the forest he sees in his own exhaustion, for the first time – How lovely the forest. Spring returns again and the fairies dance for May time madness. Dance and leap for joy, and laugh amongst roses, violets and daffodils. And the world passes by in silence bowing its head, as all the gifts of Heaven descend to enfold them under golden glory! Isn't that wondrous? And then the hunter falls asleep and the new little vixen appears and plays as before, and the frog jumps on the man's chest, and he wakes and this time the question – will he seize the vixen, or will he let her live in peace, what he has learnt from love, from life itself? (*Eagerly*) This time it's different. This time life has taught him something. He says he's going to treat the little vixen with more care, with love, he's going to break the whole endless cycle of abuse of nature. He's going to *cherish* her. Everything has to be different. It must be.

ELLIE *reaches and suddenly switches off the music. Silence. She pours herself another drink.*

JILL: Is Henry back?

ELLIE: No.

JILL: But it's nearly two. God, I hope the set hasn't fallen down. I should have been there. Ellie, you wouldn't just pop down the hall and see what's-

ELLIE: Sure, why not, it's the middle of the night, I'm pissed as a fart, Marlon Brando's pinched my bike, whoops sorry, our bike. So ye' of course, boss, I'll be on my way. Don't wait for up me. I may be gone sometime. (*Doesn't move*)

JILL: I'm sure he'll be fine.

ELLIE: Well, he's survived a battlefield. I don't think Buxton's going to be too tough for him, do you?

JILL: I wasn't thinking of him actually, I simply meant…

ELLIE: Right.

JILL: (*Pause*) So have you thought…

ELLIE: About what?

JILL: What you're going to wear?

ELLIE: For what?

JILL: For the opening tomorrow.

ELLIE: Who gives a fuck? It's hardly Leicester Square.

JILL: No, but… you're not thinking of going in your motorbike jacket?

ELLIE: Well, how else are we going to get there?

JILL: I've ordered a taxi. Thought we could go in style. So you know I'm just saying it's a chance to wear something nice. There's a bit of reception party thing after.

ELLIE: I don't want to go.

JILL: What?

ELLIE: I don't want to sit for hours through some daft bloody opera.

JILL: So why you sitting here listening to it now?

ELLIE: Not going.

JILL: You're just tired.

ELLIE: *I'm* tired? Pot calling the kettle black.

JILL: Ellie, please, I need you there. I couldn't have done any of this without your support. I really want you there. To say thank you.

ELLIE *turns to stare at her. The sound of the approaching motorbike. Its headlights cut through the window catching* JILL *for a moment like a hare in the light. She puts her hand up to protect her face. The motor and light cut out.* JILL *backs off into the shadows as –*

HENRY *enters. He sees* ELLIE *first.*

HENRY: You waited for me then?

ELLIE *turns back to glance towards* JILL.

JILL: Well, we were getting a bit worried.

HENRY: (*Pauses*) Nowt to fret about. Just the technical stuff took longer than I thought.

JILL: Well, well done.

She smiles at him.

HENRY: You an't told her.

JILL: (*Quietly*) Told me what?

ELLIE: Go to bed, Jill. Tomorrow'll be a long day.

HENRY: Why an't you told her?

ELLIE: (*Sharply*) Why should I have told her? Why does everything have to be spoken?

JILL: What you talking about?

ELLIE: I'm not talking, that's the whole point. Just go to bed!

HENRY: You can't just pretend.

JILL: Pretend what?

HENRY: That it never happened.

JILL: What never happened?

HENRY: Me and Ell. We're lovers.

Silence. JILL *is transfixed. Eventually –*

ELLIE: (*Quietly*) How can you say that?

HENRY: Because we are. 'Cos you, me, we made love.

ELLIE: Is that what it was?

HENRY: You want to deny it? What do you want to call it then? Come on. (*Pause*) I love you. And you love me.

JILL: She doesn't… she can't…

ELLIE: Everybody knows what I feel better than me.

JILL: You… I'm sorry… you… you two… no, no way, it… How… how long as this been going on?

ELLIE: It hasn't been going on.

JILL: You fucked him?

ELLIE: Words.

HENRY: She din't do it to hurt you.

JILL: Not hurt me? Oh, so… when you… (*To* ELLIE) what were you thinking, did you imagine I'd… what rejoice with roses… and daffodils… what?

ELLIE: Jill, it's not –

HENRY: We didn't think about you at all. Sorry, but that's what love is.

ELLIE: Is it?

HENRY: Ellie, you have to admit this.

ELLIE *turns to look at him.*

ELLIE: What am I admitting to?

JILL: You fucked him!

HENRY: You love me.

ELLIE *stands speechless in front of them.* JILL *suddenly cries out in pain, and clutches her stomach.* ELLIE *rises and moves to her.* JILL *puts out her arm to stop her and suddenly retching runs off into the night.*

HENRY: Let her go. It's hard but it has to be. Come on, Ell, face up, she were never going to be your maid of honour.

Silence.

ELLIE: I've got to go to her. She's in pain.

HENRY: So am I.
ELLIE: You don't know her.

HENRY: P'raps I do. Better than you. She's a killer, Ellie, believe me.

Silence. He makes a move towards her. This time she turns away and goes out after JILL. HENRY *is lost, then picks up the shotgun. Fade to black.*

Scene Eight

The clearing in the forest.

JILL *is huddled up, sobbing. As* ELLIE *enters to her.*

JILL: Was it here? Was it here?

ELLIE *remains silent.*

JILL: (*Suddenly digging up the last dregs of anger energy*) He'll destroy you, you know, he lies, he's not true, he's... what could he see in you, I don't mean, I know what *I* see but that's not... he's taking over. Everything... he's going nowhere... he's here to stay... what are you waiting for, both of you, me to die... no problem, I'm dead already... Don't leave me.. no leave, you can't stay here, I won't have.. whatever he is scheming you can't... I trusted you with my life... and now, did I hurt you in some way, did I... yes, yes, I patronised you it's true but that's only because I was weak, I needed some place I could pretend I was strong, I didn't mean to... I'm sorry, I'm so sorry... do you know, have you any idea, how much I loved you?

Silence. ELLIE *kneels by her.*

ELLIE: Let me hold you. Let me hold you.

JILL *looks up at her. Silence.*

ELLIE: Please.

ELLIE *reaches out, turning her face towards her. At first* JILL *tries to turn away, then allows herself to be turned to face* ELLIE. ELLIE *strokes her face, then quietly leans forward and kisses her. Silence.* ELLIE *kisses her again.* JILL *sighs, then they embrace.*

A shadow beyond. HENRY *loads the shotgun. The click echoes. But the two women do not seem to hear.*

Blackout.

End of Act One

Act Two

Scene One

Outside the farm.

Music: Janacek, the meeting with Mr Fox.

The sun burns through the trees. JILL in kimono. She plays with the two masks on her hands as though a puppeteer.

JILL: Good morning, Mr Fox. (*Pause*) You say such things. You are so kind. You flatter me. (*Half singing*) Could it be- am I really beautiful? Am I really... (*Smiles*) (*To herself, more softly*) Perhaps, perhaps I am rather pretty. Oh, what are these feelings I feel now?

She puts her hand to her heart, almost fainting, then turns to see ELLIE has entered from the house. She's already dressed in T-shirt and jeans. JILL stands embarrassed/ smiling, then switches off the CD.

ELLIE: You okay?

JILL *nods.*

ELLIE: Catch your death.

JILL: No. Summer has arrived.

ELLIE: Bit late.

JILL: (*Smiling*) Never too late.

ELLIE *looks around.*

JILL: No sign of him. His room was empty.

ELLIE: Where's he gone?

JILL: Nowhere. He cometh from nowhere and unto nowhere

he hath returned.

ELLIE: When I woke up, you were gone.

JILL: I wanted to greet the sun.

ELLIE: I'll make you some brekky.

JILL: I'll make yours. (*Rises*) (*Smiling*) But don't get carried away. I don't want you to think it sets a precedent. (*Pause*) Nothing that much really has to change, has it?

ELLIE: No.

An embarrassed moment.

JILL: So? (*Pause*) Good morning.

She kisses ELLIE on both cheeks. Then manages a light kiss on the lips. She stifles a giggle. Then looks back again at ELLIE. Silence. ELLIE smiles and reaches to her face. A shot rings out, ricocheting around them. JILL almost collapses. ELLIE is already on the alert. The dying fox screams out in agony, chorused by the panicky chickens. JILL's trembling starts all over again. ELLIE puts her arm around her, protectively.

HENRY enters with the dead fox, still twitching. ELLIE is strangely attracted by it. JILL finds no sympathy or interest in it now it is dead.

HENRY: I got him before he did any more damage.

JILL: Take it away.

HENRY: Sorry, I won't –

ELLIE: Let me see him. Give him to me.

As he holds it out.

ELLIE: He's still moving.

HENRY: They do, for a time. Like the chicken when you cut off its head.

JILL: We've never done that.

ELLIE: Not yet.

She carefully takes it from him.

HENRY: Careful. There's blood.

ELLIE: Of course there's blood.

HENRY: And watch out for the fleas. They'll want a new home soon as he cools.

ELLIE: He's still hot.

JILL: (*Attempting to recover*) Well, I suppose we ought to say…

HENRY: What?

JILL: Thank you.

HENRY: No, no, I just wanted to do something by way of… I owe you, and… I know I made a fair pratt of meself.

JILL: We all did.

HENRY: You want me to skin him for you?

JILL: (*Mildly*) I don't think either of us would be seen dead wearing fox fur. But if you want to take it off and sell it, be our guest.

ELLIE: No.

HENRY: No. I woun't dream… (*To* ELLIE) But I could stake him out for you.

ELLIE: Why?

HENRY: The smell 'd warn off all the others.

ELLIE: No. (*Pause*) He's too beautiful.

She almost cries. He moves towards her. She puts up her hand.

HENRY: You've blood on your hand.

ELLIE: No problem.

HENRY: You want me to get shut of him?

ELLIE: No. I'll bury him

JILL: With full military honours.

ELLIE: (*Softly*) Ye'.

HENRY: (*Pause*) I'd best be off then.

JILL: Hold on. What about the show tonight?

HENRY: Oh, I'll not let you down with that. I'll camp up in the copse for a couple of days.

JILL: Don't be silly. It might rain.

HENRY: I've done it before.

JILL: I'm not having you on my conscience. Go fetch your stuff back. Your room's still there. Then come Sunday well we'll help speed you on your way.

HENRY: Are you sure?

He looks at ELLIE. *She looks up from the fox.*

ELLIE: (*Shrugs*) It's not my place.

JILL: As much as it's mine.

HENRY: I won't be no bother. I only make a fool of myself the once.

JILL: We all make mistakes. Read the wrong signs, go down the wrong way, and it's all too easy to get caught up in friendly fire. Isn't that right? So for the record, I just want to be very clear. Ellie and I, we love each other. We are lovers. I know it can be confusing, (*Smiles*) I was confused. We both were, but… Sometimes we struggle against what we are, who we are, we do things, they're not meant to hurt others, but … (*Looks at* ELLIE) And all we can say is, we are sorry. We're just human. Sorry. There.

She smiles. He turns to look at ELLIE.

JILL: Go on. Then we'll get some food in you. You've a show to open.

He goes.

ELLIE: Is this some kind of game?

JILL: I just want to show how much I trust you.

ELLIE: It's a test?

JILL: No. No. The opposite. It's a proof.

ELLIE: Of what?

JILL: How much we love each other.

ELLIE: I don't need proof.

JILL: Neither do I.

ELLIE: Then what's the point? It only torments the lad. He thinks he loves me.

JILL: Nothing happened between you two. Not really. Nothing profound. I know that. I understand, but it's not surprising that he doesn't. But he has to learn.

JILL goes inside. ELLIE gently strokes the fox.

ELLIE: No. No.

She whispers over the fox. It is almost a keen. Fade to blackout. The keen fuses with the distant lament of the vixen.

Scene Two

Outside the farmhouse.

Early evening. As the sunset slowly turns blood red. HENRY, stripped to his vest, is washing from an old bowl. He is humming to himself, more cheerful than one might have expected. As JILL appears from the house — she's in her South American catalogue best, tidy, tasteful. There's even a trace of make-up. The fox is to one side, with the shotgun.

JILL: Sorry about this. Once women get in the bathroom.

HENRY: Us backstage don't have to get dolled up anyway.

Good job, 'cos I've got nought decent. You look nice.

JILL: Nice. Yes, well, I would, wouldn't I? Nice. (*Getting over her irritation*) So what will you do? Will you go back to the army?

HENRY: I've to finish my walk first.

JILL: The walk to nowhere.

HENRY: Yes.

JILL: (*Eventually*)(*Carefully*) Ellie. She's easily confused, you understand that, don't you? That's why sometimes there can be… silliness.

HENRY: But she in't confused with you?

JILL: No, not anymore.

ELLIE *enters. For the first time she is wearing a dress. It's inexpensive, but elegant in style, if bordering on the brazen. Her hair is groomed, and she is wearing makeup. The effect on both* JILL *and* HENRY *is stunning.*

ELLIE: (*Stopping*) What?

JILL: What do you mean what? What are you doing?

ELLIE: Wha'?

JILL: What are you wearing?

ELLIE: What?

JILL: Will you stop saying what?

ELLIE: You're saying it as much as me.

JILL: It's the dress.

ELLIE: Ye'?

HENRY: It looks a picture.

JILL: Don't be ridiculous. It looks like some tart in a Soho bar.

ELLIE: What?

HENRY: Oh, come on! You look great, Ellie.

JILL: You don't understand.

HENRY: P'raps I do.

ELLIE: Understand what?

JILL: Why are you wearing that?

ELLIE: It's just a dress.

JILL: Just is about right.

ELLIE: You said it was a smart do.

JILL: You can't wear that. Go and change.

ELLIE: I don't have anything else. It's all I've got.

JILL: Where the hell did you get it? Go and change.

HENRY: Don't listen to here. I think –

JILL: We don't care what you think. This has absolutely nothing to do with you.

HENRY: An't it? Are you sure?

Act Two

Silence.

HENRY: Go on. Ask her. Ask her who she's wearing it for.

ELLIE: I am here you know.

Silence.

ELLIE: So what?

JILL: You heard him. Who are you wearing it for?

ELLIE: It's my only dress.

JILL: That's not an answer.

ELLIE looks between the two of them.

ELLIE: (*Eventually*) It's for you. For your opening.

JILL smiles, unaware that behind her HENRY is hardly bothered by this reply. He picks up his jacket.

HENRY: I'd best be down there. Get set up. (*To ELLIE*) I'll see you later.

ELLIE: Yes.

He goes. JILL sighs with relief.

JILL: Sorry.

ELLIE: What was all the fuss about?

JILL: Sorry… it was just… (*Grimaces*) Actually, you look a treat. Beautiful. (*She pushes ELLIE to one side and straightens the shoulder of the dress*) Perhaps a teeny bridge too far. Don't want to overexcite the natives. (*Pause*) I think I have something might just do the trick.

She leaves the room. ELLIE is alone. She moves in her dress like someone trying to discover the shape of their skin. Gently. The motorbike revs up. She's suddenly all attention. She listens to it fade into the distance. She turns the dead fox. Her hand hovers over it. She lifts it to her breasts. She slides it around her neck. It seems to burn the side of her neck that he had kissed her on. She's trembling, surprised at the sweat that runs down between her breasts. As she hears JILL returning she puts it down. JILL returns with a cashmere shawl.

JILL: It'll go beautifully with what you've got.

She puts the shawl around the neck of the compliant ELLIE, neatly covering up her cleavage.

JILL: Perfect.

As JILL re-arranges it around her neck from behind –

JILL: What's that smell?

ELLIE: It's the fox. (*Pause*) He gets everywhere.

Blackout.

MUSIC: Janacek, final section, 'Hey. But I can't see the vixen there'. Followed by applause.

Scene Three

Outside the farm.

Night. ELLIE is lighting lamps. JILL is in full celebration mode, and swigging a bottle of cava. Dancing and singing to the music.

JILL: (*Laughing*) Oh, but didn't the little children look wonderful? It broke my heart when the cubs gathered round their dead mother.

ELLIE: (*Disturbed*) But I don't get it. She got killed by accident? The hunter didn't even know he had shot her. Her death didn't mean anything.

JILL: No, her death didn't, no. But her life! Her life had meaning.

ELLIE: How?

JILL: Her life gave birth to other life. The endless cycle of life, death, rebirth. That's what the last scene is all about – the hunter realises when he sees the new young vixen that he may grow old and wither away, but the wondrous cycle of life will go on for ever.

ELLIE: But me and you, Jill, what do we have to leave? We don't have kids.

JILL: I felt I did, I was so proud of our young ones, the little vixens in my masks, the funny frog, they are the future, forget the soprano warbling away, they are the future, and we are part of it –

ELLIE: Not me. I didn't feel that. That's not what I felt... I felt...

She's on the verge of tears. She sits. She's breaking down against her own will. JILL puts a supportive arm around her. The sound of the approaching bike. ELLIE desperately ashamed of this emotional outburst struggles to recover her composure.

HENRY enters. Silence. He stands watching them. ELLIE carefully extricates herself from JILL. The sound of the vixen screaming nearby. JILL cries out, and now ELLIE turns to support her, but finally decides not to.

ELLIE: I thought he was dead.

HENRY: It's his mate. She's wild for her love. She can smell him. Smell the death of him.

JILL: What will she do?

HENRY: She'll tear the place to hell no matter what your opera says. She'll kill for the sheer spite of it now.

ELLIE: Can an animal want revenge?

HENRY: It's in her soul. Something's been ripped away and so she'll make someone pay. They're no different from us.

He grabs the shotgun.

JILL: And take the dead one with you, it stinks the place out.

HENRY: Aye, I'll use it to trap her. She'll come on his scent. That's her mistake.

He turns and is about to leave –

ELLIE: I'll come with you.

HENRY: Wha'?

ELLIE: I want to be there. I want to see her.

JILL: You'll be in the way.

ELLIE: I want to see her, face to face.

HENRY: Come then.

JILL: Don't be silly, Ell. You're hardly dressed for the jungle patrol. Look at you. Look at your shoes.

ELLIE: (*As she kicks her shows off*) I'm with you.

JILL: You've nothing on. You'll catch a cold.

ELLIE: It's a beautiful night.

She throws down the shawl and picks up her leather coat.

ELLIE: Let's go.

HENRY leaves.

JILL: (*Desperate*) Ellie, please, what are you playing at?

ELLIE: I have to go.

JILL: To what? To him – is that it?

ELLIE: I have to go.

JILL: You're killing me, you know that. Why are you doing this to me?

ELLIE: You don't understand. How could you? I don't neither, not really. Except…

JILL: What?

ELLIE: (*Quietly*) I know what I want.

JILL: (*A beat*) He's taken you over, can't you see that! Please, Ellie, please!

A beat. ELLIE leaves. JILL picks up the shawl and wraps it around her own shoulders. She cries, her cries merging with that of the vixen's. Darkness.

Scene Four

The clearing in the forest.

HENRY *is kneeling, gun at the ready. As* ELLIE *approaches. He turns to face her. He seems almost frightened.*

HENRY: Why you come after me? It in't for the fox is it?

She looks at him.

HENRY: Some kind of game? A game for grown-ups is it, not for the like of kids like me. This how you lot get your kicks? Bit of prick teasing and back to the princess all warmed up? Is that what I am? Just a bit of a giggle for the gals?

ELLIE: (*Quietly*) Don't.

HENRY: You any idea how that makes me feel? Do you care- or you just figure he's got no feelings, he's a bloke, his blood dun't run like ours, don't boil up with love, don't bleed, well, I bloody bleed. Different I don't know perhaps it is different from a woman but it's still blood. What the fuck do you care? I'm the enemy aren't I? That it? Don't waste no time dreaming of what he might be.

ELLIE: (*Softly*) Did you dream of the enemy over there? Did you dream of what they were feeling?

HENRY: (*Pause*) I do now.

ELLIE: Yes. I know you do.

Silence.

ELLIE: Why did you lie?

HENRY: 'Bout what?

ELLIE: You told her we'd made love? Why say that? Was it just revenge, was it to try to drive her mad?

HENRY: (*A pause*) Why din't you deny it? Go on, answer. (*Silence*) Must I tell you why? 'Cos it were the truth.

ELLIE: We didn't even touch.

HENRY: Come on, when you looked at me it happened. I wan't imagining. That's the truth in't it? It happened. That's what you're running from. It happened inside. Look at me. Go on, deny it. Or go on. Run.

ELLIE: (*Eventually*) I'm not running.

She looks at him. Silence.

ELLIE: You are beautiful.

She slowly moves towards him. Finally he looks away. She puts her hand up to his face, turning him, forcing him to look at her.

ELLIE: Don't be frightened.

She embraces him. Music plays under the following scene.

Scene Five

Outside the farm.

Although it could be anywhere. JILL is crouched, knees up, fighting sleep.

JILL: They talk, everybody talks. Love. Free love. What's love got to do with freedom? Nothing. I mean, you have to fight, you need to protect, you want to keep what you have, there has to be fences around the hens for *their* sake. You can't just mumble on meaningless about love, freedom, and leave the door wide open, welcome stranger, no, much as you might dream. Love must be protected, love must be secured. Love must be fought for. (*Shivers*) She can't really want… why? Why would she, sacrifice herself to… to rub her skin against the rough bark of a birch tree. Sacrifice… I can't… I won't live alone… why submit to his will? I will redeem you. And burn your dress on a midnight pyre. (*Giggles*) Yes.

She rises unsteadily to her feet.

Scene Six

The clearing in the forest.

The two entwined, half-dressed. Near to dawn. Red sky in the morning. Shepherd's warning. HENRY *laughs.*

ELLIE: What?

HENRY: You didn't really think…?

ELLIE: Crossed my mind.

HENRY: That I were after the farm? Come on, I don't care buggerall for it. I'm norra farmer. Norra soldier really. If truth were told I don't know what I am.

ELLIE: I do.

HENRY: Go on, let me in on the secret.

ELLIE: (*Shakes her head*) You can't. It's something you can't. Well, I dunno a poet maybe but… no… try as you might, you can never really get people to see what you see in them. Well, I can't anyway. Much as I'd like to.

HENRY: It's enough you love me.

Silence.

HENRY: Anyway, you knew it wan't the farm. Deep down. You knew all the time.

ELLIE: You're so sure of yourself aren't you? So cocksure?

HENRY: Man's supposed to be. Not much use else.

ELLIE: That's right is it?

HENRY: Come on, admit it. You knew what I were after.

ELLIE: Perhaps. Ye'. But, sorry, pal.

HENRY: What?

ELLIE: (*Smiling*) No way. No way you're getting my bike. Anything else but… some things are too precious.

He laughs and embraces her.

HENRY: You keep your bike. I'm not ashamed to write pillion. And we'll ride off into the setting sun.

ELLIE: To where?

HENRY: Anywhere. Nowhere. It dun't matter. As long as us two are together.

She stares at him, and then turns away.

HENRY: What is it?

ELLIE: (*Struggling*) I do… I wish… I wish I could say what I … that I could give you like a present what I see in you, to… (*Shakes her head*)

HENRY: Lost me.

ELLIE: Words.

HENRY: What you talking about, you talking about loving?

ELLIE: I don't know. It's a feeling. A feeling in me I can't make anyone see. Makes me want to cry.

HENRY: Why?

ELLIE: I dunno. (*Pause. Shakes her head*) The waste.

He tries to hold her.

HENRY: You don't need to talk about love.

As he embraces her with increased passion.

ELLIE: Please, don't. Please.

She turns away, trying to adjust her clothing.

HENRY: What's up?

ELLIE: It's not easy for me.

HENRY: What? Talking about love, or loving?

ELLIE: It's just… isn't all this, isn't it, I dunno, supposed to be freedom?

HENRY: It is freedom on a 1200 c.c... kick start, and away we go, love.

ELLIE: No, been there, done that, it's not. You end up handcuffed to the handlebars. You end up being... (*Shakes her head*) It isn't freedom.

HENRY: I'm not planning to lock you up.

ELLIE: But you are planning for me aren't you?

HENRY: For us.

Silence. She tries to get up. He grabs her wrist. She stares at his grip. He lets go.

HENRY: Come on, Ellie, it's love, whatever shape or form it comes in, this is love. What do you call what we just did if you can't use that word?

ELLIE: It happened. Just happened.

HENRY: What do you mean it just happened? You make it sound like some accident. Just one of them things.

ELLIE: No, it's not an accident.

HENRY: What is it then, fate? Has to be. I wanted you, I were never going to give up. Never. Not from the first to last. And I knew I knew you wanted me. And you did. You said you did.

ELLIE: (*Eventually*) It wouldn't have happened otherwise.

HENRY: So where do we go from here?

Silence.

ELLIE: You've said that as well. (*Pause*) Nowhere.

She sits up and begins to get dressed.

HENRY: (*Horrified*) What do you mean by nowhere?

ELLIE: I can't leave her, Henry. The poor girl. She can hardly make herself a cup of tea. She needs me.

HENRY: That in't your problem. This is your life we're talking about here.

ELLIE: This is my life.

HENRY: What you going on about? You'll let her take you over? What is she, she's some bride of Dracula, sucking the blood out of you.

ELLIE: Those are films for young men, full of fear.

HENRY: Come on, she's a bleeding witch.

ELLIE: She's just a human being, same as me and you.

HENRY: Not the same. No way. We've got love. Real love. You have to have love at the centre of everything or you're wasting your life. You have to be prepared to fight for it. Not just lie down and let that bitch slide all over you.

ELLIE: I don't want to fight.

HENRY: What is this, some kind of sister thing?

ELLIE: Don't get me wrong. It's not for the sex. It's not that for either of you. Sex is… (*Shakes her head*) I'm not saying I don't love you, I'm not saying I don't love her. Not saying I do, but the pair of you are so certain of what Ellie wants, well, I'm not…

HENRY: So you just lie down for whoever wins?

ELLIE: Oh, come on, listen to yourself –

HENRY: Well, I'm in for the fight.

ELLIE: So what are you going to do, the pair of you, pistols at dawn? Why can't either of you get it into your head – this isn't some fight for fair lady.

HENRY: You're dead wrong there. That's exactly what it is. I love you too much to stand back and watch you destroy yourself.

ELLIE: (*Sharply*) Don't go making decisions on my behalf.

HENRY: But you can't make them for yoursen.

ELLIE: In time. In *my* time.

HENRY: Meanwhile, she sucks your blood. Soon you'll be as knackered as she is, and she'll be the one tap dancing on your grave. I'm not going to be standing there weeping, knowing what I should have done.

ELLIE: (*Suddenly near to tears*) You're so young. I can't do anything to save you. It's not my fault you are so young. And that you are so beautiful and so stupid. There's nothing wrong with that. It's only natural.

HENRY: (*Almost in tears*) And what's your excuse for being stupid?

ELLIE: (*Pauses*) Every time I learn something from life, life's different. (*Shakes her head: it's the best she can do*) Do you understand me?

She reaches out to him. He is furious, shakes her off.

ELLIE: I don't want to hurt anybody. But what can I do?

The vixen cries out. He pushes ELLIE *away and picks up the shotgun.*

ELLIE: Leave her be. Let her live! Let her end her days singing to her cubs.

HENRY: And what will you do? Feed the bitch chicken wings on a silver platter? Bloody stupid!

ELLIE: Henry!

He goes off. She's shaking.

ELLIE: You are stupid. You are. And cruel, Ellie. You shouldn't have done… done what… I couldn't help. With him. With her. Different. I didn't mean to hurt, did I? I didn't mean to fight. I just… what? Come on. What are you doing, Ellie? And why? (*Shakes her head*) Forgive me. Forgive-

A shot rings out, followed by a tortured cry that could be fox, could be human.

ELLIE: (*Softly*) Oh, no. No. Dear Jesus. No.

The crying stops. Silence. As HENRY *appears. He no longer carries the shotgun.*

HENRY: I just heard a cry. Then… a shiver, a…. the bush…. a movement, then all I saw… just the eyes, it was all so dark. How could I know? How could I have known?

She turns to rush out. He grabs hold of her. He holds her as she struggles.

HENRY: Don't. Don't. There's nought to … You mustn't see… please… you mustn't see…

He cries out then clings onto her as he collapses.

HENRY: It wasn't me, I didn't… how was I to know? She must've been trying to spy on us, hiding out in the bushes. I just heard the cry caught the movement and I thought I don't know I thought I saw her eyes and…. you can't wait…. the fox don't wait you understand, you're no time to… and you either fire or pass, and one of you is either alive or dead… Mistakes…. Happen… I didn't mean to… mistakes… friendly fire… I was only trying to protect, you understand, only… Oh God, dear God.

As he crumbles, she holds him as in a pieta, and slowly begins to keen over him as if it was he who was dead. Time passes.

ELLIE: (*As if to a child*) It'll be… it'll be….

Silence.

HENRY: It's an accident. They can't charge me for that. They couldn't charge me before. These things happen. It's the countryside. How was I to know she were hiding… why would I have even imagined… but it'll be all right won't it? Nobody could think… why would they?

She stops stroking him and remains immobile.

HENRY: (*Trying to rally round*) It happens. It's terrible. But that's life. We have to go on. We'll be together.

As he kneels now by her. She rises.

HENRY: What you doing?

ELLIE: Going to her.

HENRY: No. You can't.

As he reaches to her.

ELLIE: (*Quietly*) Don't touch me.

She leaves. HENRY stands terrified. A sound echoing the vixen of ultimate pain. ELLIE returns. She's carrying the shotgun. She looks as though she is about to faint. He makes a movement towards her. She holds the shotgun up at him. He looks away.

ELLIE: Look at me.

HENRY: What?

ELLIE: Look at me, Henry.

He's baffled. She points the shotgun.

ELLIE: Look me in the eye.

He looks at her. Finally he looks away. She is crying silently.

HENRY: Are you going to shoot? This is it, this is the time, if you're going to shoot? (*Pause*) What I did, whatever I did, I did for you. Go on, come nearer, accidents happen. Come on, real close, make it look like a suicide. Give me the gun. Let me do it. I'm dead already inside.

Silence.

ELLIE: It doesn't matter. It really doesn't matter. (*Pause*) Go.

He waits a moment but it's as if she no longer sees him. Finally, he goes. She's hardly able to stand in the shadows. ELLIE slowly, in shock, makes her way automatically to —

Scene Seven

Outside the Farm.

As the first sign of dawn. ELLIE sits at the table and puts the gun down. She stares at the CD player then slowly, almost hypnotically, switches it on. MUSIC: Janacek, the opening prelude music. She listens then looks around, as though searching for the animals and insects in real life. She switches off the music and then becomes gradually aware of the real dawn chorus as it begins. In the distance the sound of the fox cubs calling. Startled, she automatically reaches out to her gun. Then stops. She stares out straight in front of her as – The dawn rises and the sun hits her eyes. She blinks for a moment, and then opens them again.

Blackout.

The End

Afterword

In 1918, D. H. Lawrence and his wife Frieda made the acquaintance of two young women in the village of Hermitage in Berkshire, out in the country to the west of London. Cecily Lambert and her cousin Violet Monk were trying to run a farm in an England denuded of men; they had goats, chickens, a marauding fox and many problems. The Lawrences befriended them; and by the end of the year, or early in 1919, Lawrence had written his story 'The Fox', which drew on many of the facts of their lives. Although Lawrence's fictional Jill Banford and Ellen March, two women running a farm, are not Cecily Lambert and Violet Monk, they were vivid recreations of them.

Lawrence's 'Fox' exists in two distinct versions. The 1918-19 story ends with the interloper Henry Grenfel proposing marriage to Ellen March, and her telling him that he reminds her of the fox which has been terrorising the farm chickens (and which he has killed). And they get married, much to Jill Banford's disapproval; she cannot bear the "half-dreamy, half-knowing look of happiness on March's face". The story ends with Henry having had to go away (he is still in the army), but determined to return: "He would come home by instinct" are the last words of the story, which was published in *Hutchinson's Story Magazine* in November 1920.

In 1921, however, Lawrence completely rewrote the ending of the story, for its publication in a volume of short novels. In the rewritten version, Henry – feeling utterly frustrated by the malign influence which Banford has on March – is responsible for Banford's death (he chops down a tree which kills her as it falls). It is his only way of getting March. He marries her, but there is then a long passage at the end of the story in which they wait for emigration to America, and the story concentrates on Henry's intense dissatisfaction. He wants March to change: not to be "an independent woman with a man's responsibility" any more. He feels he will not come into possession of his own life "till she yielded and slept in him". The story is at the end almost entirely concerned with Henry's point of view; his desire not just for the woman but to leave England. It is a strange and (to me) difficult and rather horrible ending. I don't want March to yield to Henry. He however wants her "surrender".

Stephen Lowe's play, he insists, does not adapt the story. And that's right. It responds to it. It does not just modernise the action while remaining for most of the time faithful to its dynamics (and achieving a wonderful and convincing update). It adds in new elements completely: the music, and the life of nature continually suggested by the music, are both very important. As in the second version of the story, Henry kills Jill – accidentally on purpose, so to speak – but the situation of a very independent Ellie March is such that it is *her* life with which we are concerned. Love, sex and marriage are not sufficient reasons for her to partner with Henry. She too wants to be independent; she knows he is young and in an odd way innocent: not a partner for life. The ending of the play, of course, is utterly ambiguous. Is she sitting, listening to the voices of re-awakening nature around her, feeling herself once more part of a larger world, not simply of the narrow human world in which people keep demanding love and she keeps wishing to withhold it? Or is she sitting there, just like Jill in being bemused by art as a substitute for the life she has in effect walked away from? Or does she sit, with the gun ready beside her, utterly hopeless about her future as an independent woman (she gave up London for this place: and now Jill is dead and Henry gone). Being Lawrentian is not just a matter of finding the right partner and going away forever (Lawrence's own story shows that too, even in its very problematic ending). It's a matter of finding your own independence, and your own place in the world as well.

What is this thing which is called the Lawrentian? It is striking how often Lawrence parodied the idea of himself that so many readers continue to think is the heart of what he did. Henry – loving, wanting, muscular, outdoors – is a parody of the Lawrentian ideal, and Stephen Lowe brings that out beautifully. What his plays also do is bring the history of the idea down to the twenty-first century.

At the end of March 1929, D. H. Lawrence and his wife Frieda spent a weekend with a rich American couple, Harry and Caresse Crosby, at the 'Moulin du Soleil' outside Paris; they had got to know them a fortnight earlier. Surviving photographs show the Lawrences sun-bathing in the courtyard, and Lawrence pottering about in a little horse-drawn buggy with Caresse. But Stephen Lowe's play goes a great deal deeper. It is concerned with the Lawrence who was trying to place his novel *Lady Chatterley's Lover* with a Parisian publisher who would make it the success that Lawrence – dying – wanted to achieve for the sake of his wife Frieda; it concerns the man who wrote that novel; and the man who knew that Frieda was regularly betraying him with the Italian army-officer Angelo Ravagli. Above all it shows the writer who just four months earlier had told Brigit Patmore (while he and Frieda were with Richard Aldington, Brigit and Arabella Yorke on the island of St Port Cros, which involved daily swimming by the four healthy occupants of the Vigie) how he used to think that he had something in his life "which makes up for everything", but had then found that he hadn't got it. Almost certainly, he meant sexual desire. To me it is miraculous that Stephen Lowe tells so much of the truth of the situation so deftly, so thoughtfully and painfully.

Biographies nearly always encourage their readers to *understand* the subject of the biography: they usually do this by telling the reader what the subject was like.

Playwrights don't do this (unless, like Shaw, they fill out huge stage directions trying to tell you what to think). Their plays have to do the work. Caresse Crosby wrote – about the weekend she and Harry saw the Lawrences at the *Moulin du Soleil* – that Lawrence was "fugitive, strung taut and full of wisdom", while Frieda was "upholstered, petulant and full of pride". Those are the very things we see. What is very moving, however, is that in a world full of sexual desires, Lawrence – the great writer about sexuality – plays almost no part. But the Lawrentian ideal is everywhere.

What a playwright needs to do is not only leave the outline facts untouched (Lawrence was 44 and dying, Frieda was having an affair with Angelo Ravagli, Cagliostro had inhabited the Moulin du Soleil, there was a "magic pond" there) but also create the people so that they enlarge to fit the spaces that biography and memoir, however accurate or spirited, always leave. The play has to make the person real. The reality of Lawrence – like the reality of Banford – is what comes over so extraordinarily.

The man is a writer. He is dying. He is not just terribly touchy, he is raw. He is concerned with finding ways of saying farewell to the things and the people he has loved, while also being determined not to give up or give in. We realise *why* he is so angry, *why* he is so rude and violently unpleasant; we don't even think of forgiving (the play is much too interesting for us to go down such moral roads) because we entirely sympathise: as we do with the Frieda who has to cope with the sick and angry Lawrence while also inevitably set on leading her own life too. Why doesn't the English language have a word for "sympathise" which does not somehow suggest that we are sorry for someone? Lawrence is much too impressive, determined, clever, sad, engaged, and a whole lot more, for us ever to be sorry for him: and that is something that the play brings out wonderfully. A few months before his visit to the Crosby couple, he wrote how

> I never saw a wild thing
> sorry for itself.
> A small bird will drop frozen dead from a bough
> without ever having felt sorry for itself.

That's the Lawrence whom Stephen Lowe brings us to realise.

John Worthen